Creative Therapies with Traumatized Children

of related interest

Communicating with Children and Adolescents
Action for Change
Edited by Anne Bannister and Annie Huntingdon
ISBN 1 84310 025 8

The Story So Far
Play Therapy Narratives
Edited by Ann Cattanach
ISBN 1 84310 063 0

Play Therapy
Where the Sky meets the Underworld
Ann Cattanach
ISBN 1 85302 211 X

Play Therapy with Abused Children
Ann Cattanach
ISBN 85302 193 8

Creating a Safe Place
Helping Children and Families Recover from Child Sexual Abuse
NCH Children and Families Project
ISBN 1 84310 009 6

The Use of Art in Counselling Child and Adult Survivors
of Sexual Abuse
Maralynn M. Hagood
ISBN 1 85302 228 4

Profiles of Play
Assessing and Observing Structure and Process in Play Therapy
Saralea E. Chazan
ISBN 1 84310 703 1

Creative Therapies with Traumatized Children

Anne Bannister

Jessica Kingsley Publishers
London and New York

First published in the United Kingdom in 2003
by Jessica Kingsley Publishers Ltd
116 Pentonville Road
London N1 9JB, England
and
29 West 35th Street, 10th fl.
New York, NY 10001-2299, USA

www.jkp.com

Library of Congress Cataloging in Publication Data
A CIP catalog record for this book is available from the Library of Congress

British Library Cataloguing in Publication Data
A CIP catalogue record for this book is available from the British Library

ISBN 1 84310 155 6

Printed and Bound in Great Britain by
Athenaeum Press, Gateshead, Tyne and Wear

Contents

List of Tables and Figures

Acknowledgements

The writing of this book, and the doctoral research that preceded it, would not have been possible without the assistance and support of many people. First, I thank Professor Colin Robson and Professor Nigel Parton of the University of Huddersfield for their expert advice and constant encouragement. I am grateful to the NSPCC for providing accommodation for the groupwork research and to my colleagues Dr Alex Leith, Helen Landowski, Louise Brown, Baseer Mir, Tim Woodhouse, Steve Towers, Janice Wilson and Sam Heywood, for their skilful facilitation of the practical work. In addition, I thank Eileen Gallagher for her excellent supervision and Dr John Casson for his creativity.

I am grateful to Di Gammage, Enid McNeill and Anna Jacobs, who contributed to the research with their viewpoints, and to staff of the library at the NSPCC, Central Office, London, and the library at the University of Huddersfield, for their professional support. Other people who contributed through very helpful suggestions are Professor Anne Ancelin Schutzenberger, Brenda Meldrum and Alison Wales.

I acknowledge that this work would never have been attempted without the previous support of all the social work and administrative staff who have worked alongside myself at the NSPCC.

My heartfelt thanks are, of course, due to all the children and young people, their parents and carers, their social workers and their teachers who have co-operated with me during the research and in previous casework. My learning from them has been immense.

Finally the active support of my dear husband, Stan, has been the spur which has encouraged me throughout all my work. To him, and to my own children and grandchildren, this work is dedicated.

Note

In order to protect the identities of children and young people mentioned in this book their real names have not been used. In addition, some details of their backgrounds may have been changed where this could lead to identification.

CHAPTER ONE

How the Regenerative Model Evolved

The 'building bricks' of the regenerative model

The effects of trauma on the development of young children were not fully understood when society discovered the extent to which children were being sexually abused. As knowledge grew regarding child sexual abuse during the final two decades of the last century, so our understanding of the damage to child development was increased. As a probation officer in 1975, I found myself working with adolescents, so-called 'delinquents', both boys and girls, some of whom were also telling me about their early physical and sexual abuse. The links between the abuse (which had seldom been reported or confirmed) and their subsequent behaviour seemed to be obvious, but there was little research on the subject. The connection with physical abuse was strongly denied by abusing parents who, while admitting the abuse, declared that it was justified punishment for bad behaviour. At that time sexual abuse was rarely discussed, was referred to obliquely by children, was denied by parents, and often by society in general. I was also working with paedophiles, but the compulsive nature of their behaviour was not recognized at the time and no treatment was deemed to be very effective.

However, as research into the subject proliferated, so did the publications. Herman (1981) brought a feminist stance to the subject of father–daughter incest, and Sgroi (1982) introduced a medical perspective to work with survivors. Finkelhor (1984) discussed research and theory in a practical way and threw some light on the motivations of abusers, while Alice Miller (1987) discussed psychotherapy, and stressed the psychological damage caused by abuse. By now working for the NSPCC (National Society for Prevention of Cruelty to Children), I found that there were links between the physically abusive behaviour of some women to their own children, and their own early physical and sexual abuse, and I published a paper on this with my colleague, Alan Prodgers (Bannister and Prodgers 1983). Many of the young mothers with whom we worked had histories of physical and sexual abuse by their own families and others had been severely neglected during their childhoods.

Having contacts with Rape Crisis groups, and working with a support group for women who had been sexually abused, gave me further insight into the extent of the damage, and the ongoing repercussions through the second and third generations. I was also finishing training as a psychodramatist and as a dramatherapist and working with many abused women, mostly in therapeutic groups. I began to incorporate play therapy into my work with abused children, so I was influenced by the work of Moreno (1977), Jennings (1975) and Axline (1969). Moreno's theory of child development plays a key part in the practice of psychodrama but it was only later that I realized that it was also the key to my understanding of the effects of sexual abuse on young children.

Devising the regenerative model

Some aspects of my model then were already in place when I undertook the task of building a new team with the NSPCC, specifically to increase knowledge of child sexual abuse, and also to work therapeutically with children and families where such abuse had occurred. My own practical work with traumatized young people and with adults who abuse, was echoed in the experience of others who joined the team. A sociological understanding of the reasons why child sexual abuse was prevalent in our society emerged from our discussions and disagreements. We believed that imbalances in power were at the root of child sexual abuse. Some team members were familiar with creative therapies and with theories of child development which I have mentioned above. It took some time, however, before the team began to realize the full extent of the damage caused by early childhood abuse within the family, and to recognize that there were some circumstances where that initial damage could be lessened (by having supportive grandparents for instance).

A creative team is more than the sum of its parts. Our team contained social workers, administrators, a psychodramatist, a dramatherapist, and a play therapist. The team changed but the mix of skills remained fairly constant. Individually we all brought some expertise, some experience, some knowledge of childhood abuse, physical, emotional and sexual. Working constantly with deeply traumatized children meant that the team relied on each other for support. We were also training new members of our team, plus other teams, so we had to keep abreast of the mass of information on sexual trauma which was being discovered constantly. We met regularly as a team and shared our skills, knowledge and experience. We also shared our ideas and our hopes and fears. Our skills, however, were difficult to measure. It was clear that abused children responded to us but it was less clear if, and how, children benefited from our work. Those who cared for the children often stated that 'difficult' child behaviours had reduced, that communication between themselves and their children was improved, and that the children looked forward to the therapy sessions. The children themselves were usually eager to attend sessions, although painful and angry feelings were sometimes released. Sometimes their behaviour appeared to regress and carers found it difficult to cope with ten-year-olds who wanted to be cuddled and rocked after they had got in touch with their own vulnerability in a session.

I found myself asking questions which I could not answer:

- *What* exactly was the therapist doing in a creative therapy session with a sexually abused child?

- *How* was this affecting the child and how was it changing child behaviour, if at all?

- If there was a lasting effect on the child, *why* was this happening?

Trying to answer these questions was the purpose of the research which I undertook later. One insight which I did have in the beginning was the realization that in the 'creative sharing' of the team we were generating something which was 'extra' to the individual skills and experience which we already had. There were similarities in the close bonds which we forged with other team members and the therapeutic bonds which we made with children. During our team sessions we were assessing and changing our own practice just as the children appeared to be assessing and changing their own behaviour in therapy sessions.

We called our work 'the interactive approach' because children and therapists were equally valued in the work, and 'action', i.e. play, was the key

The Regenerative Model

Phase One – Assessment

Development	**Attachment**	**Coping strategies**	**Safety**
Embodiment play	Interaction child/carer	Internal/external locus of control, dissociation	Home situation
Projected play	Sociograms		Self-protection
Role play			

Phase Two – Action

Building attachment	**Creativity**
Acceptance	Interactive play
Boundaries	Child centred
Body/mind connections	Drama (role play, rehearsal)
Balance of power	Art, music, poetry, dance, story
Confirming feelings and identity	Doubling, mirroring and role reversal
Witnessing	

Phase Three – Resolution

Self-redevelopment

Ability to understand and express feelings

Awareness of self-identity

Ability to make, maintain or terminate relationships

Figure 1.1 A model for working with children who have been sexually abused

to the therapy. We soon became aware, however, that some children seemed less able to benefit than others. We looked at our own vulnerability within the therapeutic team, and realized that we could not contribute fully to our discussions unless we felt safe from judgemental reactions. So we assumed that children felt the same, in therapy. We also realized that we needed support from people outside the team (family and friends) in order to function fully, away from the work setting, and so we assumed that the children did too.

We therefore put in place an assessment procedure which later became the basis of Phase One of the regenerative model (see Figure 1.1). The philosophy behind the model is explained fully in Chapter Eight, but practically, we looked at children's development using a dramatherapy theory of play (see later in this chapter) and we decided whether their play included embodiment, projected and role play. Children enjoy embodiment play such as sandplay, clay and modelling, messy finger painting, and water play from a very early age, and projected play with dolls, puppets or drawing and painting materials is usually included within their first two years. Role play may begin at any time after that (including 'dressing up') and usually by five years children are accomplished in play at all levels and include some of each over a series of sessions. Many of the children that we saw were stuck in embodiment or projected play and it seemed that their development had been impaired or delayed at an early stage. Often the abuse could be traced to early beginnings at this crucial stage of development. We knew from experience that these children took much longer to show some signs of recovery.

Also during the assessment procedure we looked at the attachments which they had to *current* carers. We also assessed attachments to former carers or parental figures. We were informed by the work of Fahlberg (1994) and Howe (1995) in particular. Children who had no secure attachments were often more difficult to engage in therapy. When an attachment was eventually made with the therapist it was still often an 'ambivalent attachment' (Ainsworth *et al.* 1978) or a 'disorganised attachment' (Main and Solomon 1986). Again, these were the children whose recovery took a greater time. We noticed, however, that children who had managed to make some kind of attachment to a current carer (often a foster parent) responded better to the therapy.

The child's coping strategies were important to assess during therapy, to ensure that these were not eroded too soon and were valued for what they were. We found that children who were abused often accommodated to their abuse by using extreme coping strategies. These were sometimes related to gender but not exclusively so. Many boys, and some girls, had become very controlling in their behaviour in order to cope with feelings of powerlessness. These were the children whose behaviour was often classed as 'unmanageable' or 'difficult'. Others, mainly girls, became stuck in their victim role and became bullied, clingy, or 'whingeing', much to their own distress and that of their current carers. It was important not to focus on a programme to reduce these behaviours too early, or the child would feel even more vulnerable. The exception to this is the child who is sexually abusing others. Obviously a behavioural programme should address this, to protect the child and others, but therapeutic work on the child's own abuse should also be run alongside, if possible.

Similarly, the use of dissociation by the child, which is a very effective coping strategy during periods of extreme stress, violence or pain, was noticed and explored, but not discouraged until the child felt safer. Safety, therefore, was the key to successful therapy, even if that meant things moved at a slower pace. The current home situation was also, therefore, carefully assessed to ensure that the child was not still in danger of abuse and that the child had some skills of self-protection in place. Great care was exercised regarding the latter. If skills of self-protection are taught at too early a stage in the therapy the child may well feel that the 'reason' for their abuse was that they had failed to protect themselves and thus their own guilt is compounded.

It will be seen from the above that the attachment process between therapist and child was assumed to be highly important (as it is in most, if not all, therapy). We advocated 'total acceptance' of the child, together with firm boundaries put in place by the therapist. Body/mind connections were always kept in mind (as in most kinds of creative therapy), as was the balance of power between child and therapist. Stress was laid on the confirmation of the child's feelings (some children were very confused and unable to experience feelings) and on confirmation of identity, which also was usually unclear. The importance of the therapist acting as a witness to the child's statements and actions was stressed.

All therapy was interactive and child centred and usually included drama, art, music, poetry, dance, story, and the psychodramatic techniques of doubling, mirroring and role reversal. Progress was determined when the therapist felt that a child had gained an ability to understand and express feelings and had some awareness of self-identity. When a child also enjoyed the ability to make, maintain and terminate relationships, it was felt that it might be possible to terminate the therapy.

It will also be seen from the above that although the therapy appeared to be largely successful, we had not fully answered our earlier questions of 'What?', 'How?' and 'Why?'. This then was the purpose of the research which I undertook later, with the support of the NSPCC. I realized that Moreno's theory of child development was crucial to my understanding of the damage inflicted by repeated sexual abuse of children in their early, developing years. I also realized the importance of the dramatherapy theory of play development in our practice and treatment. These two theories, together with the whole concept of play and its importance in development, were the key factors in our practice. During the so-called 'decade of the brain' (1990s), my subsequent understanding of the neurological effects of abuse in a child's developing years provided great insight into the reasons why children are so damaged by it. My research enabled me to bring together all these factors to produce the regenerative model for working with abused children.

Moreno's theory of child development

Moreno suggested that children's development depends on their environment, and particularly on their parents or carers. His theory of child development was published in 1944 (Moreno and Moreno 1944) and later refined in 1952 (Fox 1987). Jacob Levy Moreno was an Austrian psychiatrist who invented the method of psychotherapy known as psychodrama. He suggested that the development of an infant is accomplished in three stages: the first stage of finding identity, the second stage of recognizing the self and the third stage of recognizing the other. He suggests that these stages are reflected in the actions of the primary carer for the infant.

For a small infant who is still in the identity stage, the primary carer will often 'double' the child to assist in the expression of feelings. For instance, mothers may talk to their babies, trying to interpret their cry and trying to put themselves in the child's place. They may suggest that the infants are cold or hungry and will try to pacify them. The expression of feelings, and some acknowledgement of this by others, helps the child to create an individual identity. Doubling is also a psychodramatic technique where one person stands alongside another (the protagonist) and, copying body language and voice tone, makes explicit feelings which are unspoken by the protagonist. These can be corrected or modified by the protagonist until a clear understanding of the protagonist's feelings is gained both by the double and by the therapist and other group members (if the work is part of a therapeutic group). This is similar to the process of one or more caregivers trying various interpretations until the baby is pacified.

The technique of doubling is central to psychodrama and it helps protagonists to clarify and express deeper levels of emotions (Blatner 1997). A special application of doubling (the containing double) is used by the psychodramatists Hudgins and Drucker (1998) when working with sexually abused adults, in order to contain the trauma. Moreno suggested that this technique is used instinctively by a competent carer who reacts to the child's cry or smile with words and actions which seek to interpret that which the infant is trying to express. This enables the child to express itself in a way which is understood, at least by the main carers and also, often, by siblings and others in the immediate environment. This confirmation of the child's identity begins at birth and continues throughout early childhood.

Once the child's identity (or personality) begins to form the main carer then automatically seeks to reflect this back to the infant by 'mirroring' behaviour. This is the second stage of development. Mirroring is also a psychodramatic technique whereby one person simply repeats the words and actions of another (the protagonist) to show them how their actions are perceived by others. This must be done in an honest way which does not mock or exaggerate. Infants are able to recognize their own reflection in a mirror at an early age and also appear to recognize reflections of their own behaviour when this is repeated by a trusted carer. (The Peek-a-Boo game may illustrate this.) For an infant, these reflective actions by an adult or a sibling help the child to see how they are perceived by others.

The third stage of child development, according to Moreno, is role reversal, when a child begins to understand that others have feelings and needs and that these may be different from those of the self. Usually by the age of three, children are playing with others and role play and role reversal figure largely in this activity. Children play at being parents, or pets, or siblings and also their play includes mythical creatures such as monsters or fairy godmothers, with which they may be familiar from stories or television. They learn to play different roles and so increase their own capabilities (or role repertoire) and also learn to interact more easily with others. The concept of sharing, for instance, is learned through the ability to role reverse with the other. This explains why most two-year-olds are unable to share. However, most children are adept at role reversal before the age of five, especially if they have had the opportunity to play with others, and thus they can share fairly well at that age.

Moreno sought to show that a child develops by social interactions. He states:

> There is still another aspect neglected in describing the development of the human infant – that of probing more deeply into such generalised terms as environment, situation or field… The most important parts, within environment or fields, are the interacting individual organisms. It is important to know how these individual organisms interact and particularly how the human infant interacts with other individual organisms. (Moreno and Moreno 1944, p.7)

Moreno postulated that where this early interaction has been missing or flawed, as in trauma situations, then the developing child may suffer damage. He also suggested that this damage may be rectified by creative therapy such as psychodrama which seeks to recreate early childhood situations, to instigate essential actions which may have been missing in childhood, and to repair or correct damaging childhood experiences.

I was intrigued by Moreno's comment which compares the comparatively short period of gestation, and the very long period of dependency of the human child, with that of most animals. He suggests that this shows the importance of the long period of dependency, which is characterized by social interactions between the child and parents or others. He estimates the period of total dependency as being the first three years of a child's life and the first six years as crucial to a child's future development.

Moreno calls his theory 'The spontaneity theory of child development', because he believes that infants require great spontaneity in order to be born. At birth the child is experiencing a totally new act which requires her to be spontaneous, to breathe, to cry, to suck and so on. This spontaneity is utilized frequently during the infant's early life, but later on children and adults seem to lose the facility to be spontaneous. Psychodrama uses spontaneity as an essential creative beginning to therapy (as does dramatherapy and play therapy) and therefore it appears to connect with the early spontaneity with which children are born.

Moreno also points out that children usually make great use of dolls or other similar figures with which to play and to understand their world. He feels that such play is much more effective if 'behind the doll there is a real, feeling person' (Moreno and Moreno 1944). He refers to such persons as 'auxiliary egos', a term he also uses to describe adults in a psychodrama therapy group who assist the protagonist (or therapee) to complete their 'act hunger' and work on personal difficulties.

In my work with abused children and with abusing parents at the NSPCC, I was able to see the generational links and to understand the extent of the damage. Working with groups of abusing mothers, I also saw how powerful metaphor, in dramatherapy, became. When I observed children playing in our day care centre I could see in action how their play reflected their developmental delays.

Dramatherapy theory of development

Other practitioners with children, such as Jennings (1993, Ch.1, and 1995, p.97), also suggested a theory of child development which is apparent in the way children play. Jennings acknowledges her debt to Moreno and also to Slade (1995) who worked with children in education. Children's first play she describes as 'embodiment' in which children find identity by playing with their own bodies and that of their carers, or with their bodily excretions and food. Later they may use clay or paints in a similar fashion. Their second play or stage of development can be described as 'projection', in which dolls and puppets are used onto which to project feelings and actions. The third stage of play is that of role play where children interact with others, as already described by Moreno. Slade discovered dramatherapy (he was the first person to use the term) as a way of helping children work through childhood difficulties and Jennings and others have refined and amplified his method.

It will be seen that these two theories (of Moreno and Jennings/Slade), although independently devised in different countries and cultures and at different periods, have many similarities. Both have been devised by people working with and observing children at play. Both expand the environmental theories which have developed since the mid-20th century.

The importance of play

I suggested earlier that I had been influenced by the ideas of Moreno, Jennings and Axline. The latter first published *Play Therapy* in 1947, but she was following in the footsteps of others who have used play as therapy. Psychodrama, dramatherapy and play therapy are all forms of play and many of those who theorize about child development have recognized the value of play and illusion. Winnicott sums up his description of play as follows:

> The child gathers objects or phenomena from external reality and uses these in the service of some sample derived from inner or personal reality. Without hallucinating the child puts out a sample of dream potential and lives with this sample in a chosen setting of fragments from external reality. (1971, p.51)

Holmes (1992, pp.154–155) suggests that psychodrama, which uses playing and illusion, serves the same purpose as play. The psychodrama space is filled with creativity, fantasy and imagination and, in addition, it contains elements of the 'here-and-now'. Jennings (1987, pp.30–31), in her first major book on dramatherapy, also connects with Winnicott's concept of play and stresses the 'area of illusion'. She reminds us of Jung's contribution of 'archetypes' to our understanding of the mind. She states that 'archetypal experience can be recognised as a valuable and enriching function, even in the adult person'. Dramatherapy uses archetypes and symbols and appears to utilize the 'third space' which play inhabits and which is used naturally by children.

In a chapter in the same volume Gersie (1987, pp.46–70) states that it is crucial that we are able to gain access to our capacity to play. She quotes Piaget (in Piaget and Inhelder 1969) whose own theory of child development included a statement that 'the child must have available an area of activity whose motivation is not adaptation to reality but on the contrary assimilation of reality to the self, without coercion or sanctions. Such an area is play...'

Some children will be able to act as their own healers through the play which they devise, either alone or with others. Those who work closely with deeply traumatized children (as I have done) also recognize that the ability to play can be disrupted if the trauma is deep and there has been no support for the child. Such traumatized children need to be helped to play again. Cattanach (1992) describes play therapy with abused children and explains her methods, which encourage individual children to play in the fantasy space which she, as the therapist, makes safe with careful boundaries.

In my own work (Bannister 1997, pp.12–13) I have explained how some children who have been severely abused find it difficult to play but how the sensitive use of creative therapy can help them to play again, and to effect their own healing. In the same book (Bannister 1997, pp.75–91) I give several examples of my work with young adolescent children whose own sexual abuse was perpetrated in infancy. These children were, however, still suffering many years later. They were unable to 'talk through' their problems even though they were supported by helpful foster parents. They were, however, able to work through the metaphors of stories, sometimes legends and fairy stories, sometimes stories which they had devised themselves. They used the stories, sometimes combined with painting or role play, to work through difficulties which were too painful to name directly. In other words they used the 'play space', the 'area of illusion', the 'space between', the intermediate space which was necessary for their development. In this space they were able to complete development which had been blocked or delayed and after these sessions they appeared to grow and progress in a more healthy way.

Child development and the effects of abuse

Research is still taking place on understanding how the effects of abuse in infancy and childhood affect development. Pynoos, Steinberg and Goenjian (in van der Kolk, McFarlane and Weisaeth 1996, Ch.14) have recorded physical symptoms in abused children, such as chronic sleep disturbances, which in turn can lead to irritability and difficulties in concentration and attention. In itself this can cause serious learning problems and also relationship difficulties. These authors also quote changes in brain activity which have been noted in various studies when 'the startle response' is induced in children (Kagan 1991; Krystal *et al.* 1989). The startle reflex becomes inhibited when children are repeatedly abused and it is suggested that this reduces their capacity for reflection, their academic learning and their focused attention. Research by the same authors also shows that abused children may live in 'a state of preparedness for negative emotions'. Such a condition also has an effect on the brain and can have a deleterious effect on general information processing.

The work of Allan Schore (1994) also throws some light on this. In his detailed and extensive descriptions of the attachment process between the primary carer and the child, he states that 'opiates play a unique role in socioemotional imprinting, and attachment developmental processes' (p.145). He describes the mechanism whereby the emotionally expressive face of the primary carer induces alterations in opioid peptides in the child's developing brain. He states that these changes (usually induced towards the end of the child's first year) make permanent morphological changes in the brain. These changes, of course, are usually positive, enabling the child to regulate his or her own emotions.

I suggest that disturbance of the attachment process, which frequently occurs when children are repeatedly abused in their early years by a person who has some responsibility for their well being, leads to a distortion of parts of the developmental learning processes. This suggestion may also go some way towards explaining why creative therapies which use techniques which echo developmental processes (for instance, the techniques of doubling, mirroring and role reversal in psychodrama) are particularly effective with those whose developmental attachment processes have been disturbed in some way. My experience in practice would seem to show that the 'permanent' changes *can* be reversed or alleviated. Schore makes it clear throughout his work that the brain is capable of 'plasticity', especially during childhood, so it seems feasible that such a reversal is possible.

In any event the desirability of a flexible treatment method or intervention with children abused in their early years would seem to be obvious. A method which is reactive to each child's expressed needs is indicated. Enabling abused children to conceptualize and express their needs is also a difficult task, which may need to be undertaken before any other reparative work can be attempted. Children who have been abused have seldom been allowed to state feelings and desires and, if they have, these have often been negated, disparaged or ridiculed. This constant denigration or emotional abuse seems to block expressiveness and creativity in many children. Some children, however, especially if encouraged outside the home, do develop creative ways of expressing their feelings, through drama, art, music and poetry, for instance. This creative expression may appear only at school, with a trusted teacher or with friends. Any treatment method, therefore, will also have to enable children to be creative and to overcome blocks to creativity and expression which may have been created by their abusers or which have been put in place by other factors in their environment.

An overview of my conclusions

- Young children who have been repeatedly abused, by caregivers or close family members, suffer damage to their development which may have long-term effects.

- Depending on the stage at which the abuse began, this damage may affect understanding and expression of feelings, understanding of personal identity and the development of empathic relationships.

- Any such damage to development may lead to future learning difficulties.

- Creative therapies can induce positive behavioural changes in abused children.

- It is likely that the positive effect of creative therapies results from their capacity to recreate developmental processes. Negative brain patterns caused by abuse may thus be reversed.

- Most children enjoy participating in creative therapy.

- The regenerative model provides a theory for effective therapeutic work with abused children and also a practical, flexible approach.

We were already aware, of course, that there were mediating factors on the effects of sexual abuse and that these had been shown by various studies, which will be discussed in the following chapter. These mediating factors could account for some differences in the relative success of creative therapies with abused children. It seemed that a majority of children could benefit from the therapy to some extent and that this depended on their personal history and their present situations. The reasons for this conclusion are explained in the following chapters.

CHAPTER TWO

Repairing the Damage

The effects of abuse

For many years the effects of sexual abuse on the child were minimized or denied (Pomeroy 1968). However, Finkelhor (1984) argued that studies such as that by Gagnon (1965), Landis (1956) and Tsai, Feldman-Summers and Edgar (1979) contained flaws in design which made the interpretation of the results questionable. These studies seemed to show that only a minority of adult women felt that they had been damaged by their childhood sexual abuse. Finkelhor's own study on this subject confirmed that of others (Herman 1981; Herman and Hirschman 1977), to show that women who had been sexually abused felt stigmatized and had low self-esteem, especially sexual self-esteem.

For over a decade there were many studies which showed links between people who were having difficulties ('troubled populations') and who also had a history of sexual abuse. The most quoted troubled populations included drug abuse (Benward and Densen-Gerber 1975), prostitution and running away (Gelinas 1983), depression and alcohol abuse (Peters 1988). Sexual abuse seldom leaves physical scars and discussions of sexual matters have traditionally been discouraged in most cultures. In addition, children's knowledge of sexuality is often restricted to their experience. If they are being sexually abused by a trusted adult, research has shown that younger children (under 12) will accommodate this into their experience and blame themselves or normalize it (Summit 1983). This 'accommodation syndrome', along with cultural reticence on discussion of sexual matters, means that children have traditionally been discouraged from telling anyone of the sexual abuse they have suffered.

A particularly interesting study (Friedrich 1988) looked at the behaviours of children who had been abused and, in particular, related this to their coping styles and how these styles are embedded in the child's environment or ecological system. Friedrich stressed that the coping styles of the parents or carers of the abused child are also important factors in the outcome for the children. This seems to me to show that many children learn to adapt and cope with sexual abuse, and that their coping styles are enmeshed with those of their parents, so that their behaviour is not necessarily seen as problematic. The adaptive behaviour is simply seen as part of the child's personality and it is only later when difficulties arise, perhaps from their excessive use of control in adolescence, for instance, that the coping strategies are recognized for what they are.

Damage to child development

1. ATTACHMENT

In a report to the World Health Organisation in 1951 John Bowlby, who had been asked to advise on the mental health of homeless children, wrote: 'What is believed to be essential for mental health is that the infant and young child should experience a warm intimate and continuous relationship with his mother (or permanent mother-substitute) in which both find satisfaction and enjoyment' (Bowlby 1969, pp.xi–xii). Bowlby's seminal work *Child Care and the Growth of Love* (1953) caused radical changes in the teaching of child development.

The importance of children's attachment to their primary carer and of the adult's bonding to the child was at last recognized, although Bowlby's focus on the mother–child relationship was shown by Rutter (1981) to be too exclusive. It was clear that children can and do attach themselves to more than one caregiver and that this is a rewarding and beneficial experience for the child. Bowlby's revelations were further extended in work by Ainsworth and her colleagues (Ainsworth *et al.* 1978). They devised an experiment where children between 12 and 18 months were left alone for a short period without their primary carers (the 'strange situation' test). This demonstrated that most children at this age were clearly attached to their mothers, although some attachments were ambivalent (where carers were inconsistent) and some were avoidant (where carers were rejecting). It will be seen that there is a link here between attachment and the 'accommodation syndrome', previously mentioned, in which children adapt to long-term damaging situations in order to minimize their own distress. Securely attached children are able to tolerate the absence of their mothers for a short period, since they are confident that she will return, and they are able to carry within themselves a positive model of both their caregivers and themselves. This ability extends into mental representations of the self, other people and the relationship between self and others (Howe 1995). Some children who have suffered trauma demonstrate a disorganized pattern of attachment where caregivers are seen as frightening or frightened and themselves as helpless, angry or unworthy. This leads to difficulties in being able, fully, to conceptualize other relationships in a different way.

Other recent writers have looked at the nature of attachment. Woodhead (1997, p.67) has stated that the predisposition to seek out enduring human relationships is a feature of the infant but it is much less clear to what degree this is linked to specific features of early nurturing environments. He stresses the cultural assumptions which have led some Western childcare writers to state that only a close relationship with one caring adult can provide a child with a good attachment base. Other cultures, where caring is shared by several family members, show different results.

There has also been some work by psychiatrists and analysts on complex models of the mind which may throw some light on the attachment process. Schore (1997a) refers to the work of Melanie Klein and in particular her well known work on projective identification, which she defined as an early developmental interactive process between two individuals, wherein largely unconscious information is projected from the sender to the recipient. Schore argues that this process arises in the mother–infant dyad and that for the rest of the lifespan it represents a process of non-verbal emotional communication between the private self of one person and the private self of another. In other words, this process is basic to child development and represents a mind–body communication, not linguistic, which may be essential in the making of close relationships, including the therapeutic relationship. Schore states that his work indicates that this transfer of affect represents transactions between the right brain hemispheres of the persons concerned. He also says that it is the vehicle for the transmission of attachment patterns. He confirms that the developing infant is sensorially and body-based, rather than cognitively, therefore I contend that bodily based experiences are an intimate and essential part of the attachment process.

Adults who sexually abuse children over long periods spend a great deal of time in building attachments with the children before they abuse them. In addition, they often seek to destroy attachment relationships with non-abusing parents. This process is known as 'grooming' the child to be abused (Bagley and Thurston 1996, Vol. 2, p.4; Colton and Vanstone 1996, p.112).

The process whereby sexual offenders abuse children is described by Finkelhor in his model of four preconditions (Finkelhor 1984, Ch. 5). He states that sexual offenders have to experience all four preconditions before they abuse:

- the motivation to sexually abuse

- the overcoming of internal inhibitors

- the overcoming of external inhibitors

- the overcoming of the child's resistance.

The necessity for the grooming process is seen as we look at the last two conditions. The abuser must overcome the resistance of the child's family members and friends before the child can be abused. Not only must the abuser find time to be alone with the child but he/she must also ensure that the child is unlikely to tell anyone. This means that any existing attachments to adults must be weakened or destroyed, often through systematic denigration of the non-abusing carers, by the abuser. The security of the primary attachment bond is the main defence against the trauma of abuse and its effects.

In addition, the abuser must overcome the child's capacity to resist abuse. It is known that some children within a family are not abused because the abuser takes the line of least resistance and abuses those children who do not protest too much (Finkelhor 1984, p.60). Abusers, therefore, often choose children who are vulnerable, either temporarily through parental incapacity or absence, or permanently because of major family problems. This vulnerability is used by the abuser to build a 'special relationship'. Children who have been abused often report a slow, sensory process, in which the abuser first touches them gently and innocuously, and then builds up to more intimate touching. In some cases, of course, abusers simply use force. Children who have witnessed their abuser using violence against others (as in domestic violence) will naturally be intimidated by such a person.

It is likely then that a child's healthy attachments are prevented or destroyed by a sexual abuser. Over time the abuser then forms an attachment with the child which is unhealthy in that the relationship is formed for the purpose of providing gratification to the abuser and not for the benefit of support and protection for the child. Herman (1998, p.51) quotes Janoff-Bulman (1985, pp.15–35): 'Traumatic events destroy the victims' fundamental assumptions about the safety of the world, the positive value of the self, and the meaningful order of creation.' Herman (1998, pp.51–52) also cites Erikson (1950) who suggested that the original experience of care makes it possible for human beings to envisage a world in which they belong, a world hospitable to human life. He stated that basic trust is the foundation of belief in the continuity of life and the order of nature. It is, of course, the betrayal of trust which is so damaging, and which causes the child to become more vulnerable to further abuse. Abused children may, paradoxically, cling tenaciously to carers who abuse them, either physically, emotionally or sexually.

I give an example of this in my own work (Bannister 1997, p.30) when I describe 'Edward', aged nine, who had been abused by a convicted paedophile, within a paedophile ring for over two years. Edward played with a yellow bear puppet and instructed me to pick up a brown monkey puppet. 'He wants to have his hair combed and all the bits smoothed out,' he said. The monkey puppet groomed the bear puppet carefully for several minutes. 'My mum used to comb my hair when I was little,' said Edward wistfully. He began to talk about his mother, who had been unable to care for him because of her own difficulties. The only closeness he remembered was the occasional hair combing. This 'grooming' was important to Edward and illustrates the fact that sensory experiences are vital to the attachment process.

The need to be attached appears to be a basic and necessary condition for early life. Winnicott (1971, p.6) gave us the concept of a 'transitional object', something to which a baby becomes attached and carries around determinedly. He states that the object 'stands for' the breast (or mother).

The child uses the symbolism of the object to represent the mother (or primary carer), such is the deep need for an ongoing attachment even when the mother is absent. As the infant is fully weaned (in every sense of the word), the transitional object gradually loses its importance and, to use Winnicott's term, is decathected.

When a child is sexually abused at an early age, over time, by someone who is either the main carer, or who is able successfully to denigrate the main carer, it seems likely that the attachment process is damaged and this will affect the child's identity or sense of self. Of course, as the example of Edward above shows, the dysfunction in the attachment process may begin before the child is sexually abused. This may be the reason for the child's vulnerability. However, attachment difficulties are usually present in severely sexually abused children, whether these were caused by the trauma of abuse or by earlier trauma.

2. IDENTITY

Bagley and Thurston (1996, Vol. 2, p.220) also point out that severe and chronic abuse can interfere with a child's attachment processes and emotional development, leading to problems with identity. This is true for physical and emotional abuse as well as sexual abuse. In adults this problem with identity may be revealed in suicide attempts (Briere and Runtz 1986), sexual adjustment problems (Finkelhor *et al.* 1989), eating disorders (Waller 1994; Waller, Ruddock and Cureton 1995), dissociation (Spanos 1994) and psychosomatic complaints (Scarinci *et al.* 1994). Like Bagley and Thurston, Friedrich (1995) has also discovered that abused children have difficulties with attachment, emotional problems due to the disregulating effect of trauma, and difficulties with identity or sense of self.

In a study of childhood antecedents of self-destructive behaviour in psychiatric outpatients (van der Kolk, Perry and Herman 1991), it was found that abuse during early childhood was strongly associated with suicide attempts and self-mutilation and abuse in adolescence was associated with anorexia nervosa. A child who is being sexually and emotionally abused by parents or carers is held captive by them as surely as if (s)he were a hostage in a war. Such children form their identity in relation to that of their abusive carers. It is unthinkable that those adults, upon whom they rely for survival, should be 'bad'. The children cope with this by designating themselves as 'bad' and their abusers as 'good'. Most abusers frequently reinforce this notion by telling the children that they are wicked or even evil (e.g. Bannister 1989, p.84). This concept, of being evil or 'possessed', is impossible to contain for most of the time and so the child dissociates and fragments the personality. Herman (1998, p.107) states that this 'fragmentation in the inner representations of the self prevents the integration of identity'. Herman also goes on to say that this complex psychopathology has been observed for many years and quotes Ferenzi (1955) who described the 'atomization' of the abused child's personality and recognized the coping strategies inherent in this.

An example from my own work is that of 'James', aged three years (Bannister 1991, p.85):

> James showed oral sex in detail, using anatomically correct dolls. He shook with terror while demonstrating with 'the daddy' and 'the little boy'. 'He's doing it to the little boy,' he cried, 'not me, not me.'

James spontaneously re-enacted this event during play in a therapy session. It had not been suggested to him by the therapist, myself, that he should do so. The session continued with James rescuing 'the little boy' and expressing his anger with 'the daddy'. It is likely that James was re-enacting his dissociation at the moment of the repeated trauma. According to van der Kolk *et al.* (1996, Ch. 13), James would be more likely to develop post-traumatic stress disorder (PTSD) and dissociated identity disorder (DID) because he spontaneously dissociated at the moment of trauma, in order to protect himself.

Sheldon (in Sheldon and Bannister 1992, p.85), a psychiatrist and psychotherapist specializing in work with adult women who have been sexually abused, states: 'In violating the child's physical and psychological boundaries, the abuser is violating her integrity, the very essence of her being, and her separateness is denied.' The effects of this assault on identity are often expressed verbally by adults abused as children. 'You don't know who you are' was probably the most frequent and poignant cry of adult women who had been sexually abused and had come to me for therapy during the years that I worked for the NSPCC.

Many adult women who came to me and my colleagues for group therapy during the early 1980s had been diagnosed as having borderline personality disorder (BPD). Herman (1998, p.125) states: 'Disturbances in identity formation are also characteristics of patients with borderline and multiple personality disturbances' (see also Waller 1994). In the early 1980s 'multiple personality' had not been accepted by psychiatrists. Multiple personality disorder (MPD) was eventually recognized as dissociative phenomena by the American Psychiatric Association (1987). Dissociative phenomena are described by them as 'a disturbance or alteration in the normally integrative functions of identity, memory, or consciousness'. MPD has now more accurately been named as dissociative identity disorder (DID). Many of the women I saw appeared to demonstrate 'splits' in personality which were inexplicable. Caring, loving mothers appeared to change into out-of-control abusers or into confused child-like victims in quick succession. The women were referred to the NSPCC because they were physically abusing their children, rather than because of their borderline personality disorders.

My colleague at the time, Prodgers, commented on the psychopathology of the physically abusing parent and made a comparison with the borderline syndrome (Prodgers 1984). He concluded that the women whom we saw had all the characteristics of borderline personality, i.e. arrested emotional development, poor self-image, emotional isolation, depressive loneliness and poorly suppressed aggression. These characteristics are also common to abusive parents (Kempe *et al.* 1962). He found also that their personal histories were similar in that both showed maternal deprivation in pre-verbal development. The psychopathology of both borderline patients and abusing parents also correlated.

It is worth emphasizing that the women who came to myself and my colleagues then were not referred because of sexual abuse, which was hardly recognized at that time. As I have said, they came because they had been physically abusing their children. However, the history that emerged was that at least three-quarters of them had been sexually abused and, of the rest, all had been physically or emotionally abused, usually over very long periods. This information comes from a check of the records of approximately 50 women, seen over about four years, which I made in 1985.[1] This check was precipitated by a series of psychodrama sessions when my client, 'Linda', a young mother, remembered (in 'flashback' iconic memories) severe physical abuse by her father during her childhood. She then remembered that she had been hospitalized on numerous occasions (in different hospitals) and she had always told medical staff that she had fallen down-stairs or tripped; she had obviously come to believe this explanation and to fit it into her narrative memory. Later in adulthood she had developed BPD and also all the symptoms of what we now know as DID. Possibly during dissociated incidents, she had physically abused five of her children, all of whom had been removed from her care. When she remembered the physical abuse by her father a check was done with her sister (a nurse), who expressed surprise that my client had 'forgotten' the truth of what had happened. She confirmed the physical abuse and said her sister had received broken limbs on more than one occasion.

It should be pointed out that this early work by Prodgers, on the similarities of symptoms between borderline personalities and those who abuse, has been confirmed and extended in that people with borderline personalities have also frequently been sexually abused (see Herman and van der Kolk 1987; Mollon 1996).

Just as James in the play therapy session mentioned earlier had a 'flashback' memory of his sexual abuse, so Linda had a similar memory of her physical abuse. In both cases the memory was recalled during a therapy session when the body was placed in a position which was reminiscent of the abuse. In James' case he was using dolls to represent both himself and the abuser, but I noticed that he was copying the body position of the 'victim' doll. Linda was huddled in a corner of the group with her hands protectively over her head. It was clear that both James and Linda had a very vivid recall of the incident (or incidents). It may be that they were experiencing what Schore (1994) calls 'flashbulb' memories which occur during high arousal states and which may be an adaptive survival technique. Herman (1992) tells us that traumatic memories are wordless and static. Most survivors of trauma state that they are 'without narrative' and may be described as a series of pictures. In other words, they are iconic memories.

In James' case he was still unable to own the experience. He stated: 'He is doing it to the little boy, not me, not me.' The abuse must have happened when he was into the projected stage of development and so he was able to use this to distance the horror and pain of the experience. Linda's abuse had occurred throughout her childhood, probably until she was in early adolescence, but she had been unable to integrate the experience and had suffered what had been described as psychotic episodes several times during her life.

Both James and Linda were 'lucky' in that they had witnesses to their abuse, a mother and sister respectively, who had been able to confirm the abusive experiences. James' mother, from a working-class family, was eventually able to ask for help from the social services to remove him from the abusive father and to obtain therapy for the child. In Linda's (middle-class) family, however, the abuse was contained and denied by all the members to a certain extent. Linda had responded with aggressive and violent behaviour during her adolescence which eventually led her to a psychiatric assessment, when the borderline personality diagnosis was given.

It is interesting that during the Second World War and after the Vietnam conflict, several practitioners reported combat neurosis which consisted of delayed recall and intrusive memories of violent battle scenes (see Turner, McFarlane and van der Kolk in van der Kolk *et al.* 1996). These reports were acceptable but similar reports by women and children of domestic traumatic events were disbelieved (see Herman 1992 for a full discussion). It seems likely that in young children such memories are iconic and inexplicable partly because of the immaturity of their brain functioning and partly because of their lack of cognitive understanding of the events. Where abuse continues into maturity the victim may construct a narrative which is a symptom of their ability to adapt or accommodate to the abuse. They may accept the 'family story', which is that the child is deserving of punishment. As a therapist with adult survivors I have frequently experienced adults who have excused their abusers on the grounds that they themselves were 'naughty' and 'probably deserved' the physical or even sexual abuse.

3. RELATIONSHIPS

One of the most common complaints of adults who have been sexually abused is a sense of isolation and has been well documented (Bagley and Young 1990; Herman 1981; Waller 1994). This is part of a wider problem of difficulties with relationships from which many adult survivors of sexual abuse suffer. Sanderson (1995, p.263) states that this isolation leads to an inability to communicate effectively. She is discussing the treatment of adult survivors but she points out that many of her clients remember that their own childhood was isolated and that their abusive parent(s) encouraged this. They also discouraged any expression of feeling by the children and a reliance on the sole opinions of their parents. Sanderson (1995) gives good advice to the partners of adults abused in childhood, reminding them that they will have to be diligent and careful in helping their partners to express their needs and feelings.

Difficulties in communication are common with severely sexually abused children. I give one such example (Bannister 1997, p.12) in a book about my work with sexually abused children at the NSPCC. 'Alison' had been diagnosed by teachers as having learning difficulties but she had not been properly assessed. Both the teachers and the educational psychologists had found difficulty in communicating with her. It was now known, largely through information given by her younger sibling, that she and her sisters had been sexually abused for many years, probably by both parents. I was able to accept her silence through one and a half sessions. I sat nursing a baby doll as she sat primly and quietly with downcast eyes, clasping and unclasping her hands. Eventually I remarked, looking at the doll, 'I think she has gone to sleep, good job we were so quiet.' Alison then jumped up and asked if she could write on the whiteboard in the room. She proceeded to behave like a teacher, controlling the sessions, informing me what questions I had to ask her and then writing her answers on the whiteboard. I had been told that she could not write her name but she did manage to communicate with me, mostly by writing, with phonetic and imaginative spelling.

Naturally this child's difficulties in communication ensured that she had no friends outside her family and it also ensured that she had been quite unable to tell anyone about her abuse. Sometimes abusers threaten children with severe punishment if they tell anyone about the abuse. They say, fairly accurately, that no one will believe them. Sometimes they bribe the children with gifts, as long as they do not tell. In fact, it is probably the case that the isolation, difficulties with communication and lack of relationships, caused by the trauma, make it impossible for the child to tell whether they receive bribes or threats or not.

Of course, this lack of close relationships is probably related to the difficulties in making attachments and the problems of identity, which I have already discussed. It is not difficult to see that early traumatic experiences of child sexual abuse affect children throughout their lives. Reparative experiences seem to be essential to allow more successful child development.

Studies of young people who have been sexually abused

One of the problems of research with adult populations who have been abused in childhood is that any subsequent symptoms or problems may be as a result of life events, subsequent to the sexual abuse. Even with children it is difficult to establish a clear causal relationship between child sexual abuse and subsequent difficulties. However, it is worthwhile looking specifically at research with young people who have been abused in order to check for early signs of problems which have been confirmed by research with adults.

Studies with young people by Friedrich (1988) and Briere and Runtz (1988) have already been mentioned but research by Ageton (1983) regarding sexual assault among adolescents is of particular interest because it was part of a large national youth survey in Canada. Most of the young people felt anger, embarrassment, depression and guilt immediately after the assaults, which were perpetrated largely by offenders known to the victims. The anger and depression continued during the two years over which the young people were interviewed. Fear of being alone was increasingly reported as were feelings of worthlessness and lack of interest in sex (amongst older adolescents). The feelings of worthlessness appear to illustrate identity problems in these young people.

A study by Bagley and Young (1995) into juvenile prostitution in Canada showed that 73 per cent of the young people had suffered sexual abuse in childhood and that this was very severe and of prolonged duration. Bagley and Thurston (1996) also found that adolescents who had been sexually assaulted were much more likely to manifest somatization, emotional and conduct disorders, and suicidal behaviours. One may speculate that young people who were prostituting themselves and those who were suffering conduct disorders were having trouble with relationships and identity and may well have had early attachment problems.

Conte and Schuerman (1988) collected data from a study which was a collaboration between the University of Chicago and the Harborview Medical Center in Seattle. Three hundred and sixty-nine children were seen, aged between 4 and 17 years. All had been sexually abused, the majority by someone well known to them. A comparison sample was also recruited. Social workers, parents or other significant others completed a child behaviour profile. The authors were cautious about results but eight behaviours were stated to be most prominent in the children. In order of predominance they are: poor self-esteem, aggressive, fearful, conscientious, concentration problems, withdrawal, acting out and anxious to please. Differences between abused and comparison children were all statistically significant. The fact that some children appeared to be conscientious appears to be a positive effect but could be a function of anxiety problems, especially anxiety to please.

Although it is a myth that children who have been sexually abused frequently become abusers, it is nevertheless true that young people who sexually abuse others have frequently been abused themselves. Kahn and Chambers (1991) found that 42 per cent of juvenile sexual offenders were known to have been sexually victimized and 47 per cent had been physically abused. Burgess, Hartman and McCormack (1987) followed up 34 children involved in sex rings. At follow-up the adolescents (who were matched with a control group of non-abused children) displayed major cognitive distortions such as dissociation to manage anxiety and stress. The authors suggest that this may lead to splitting of psychological and sensory experiences and that abused youths who become abusers have massive blocking of sensory, perceptual and cognition mechanisms.

Ryan *et al.* (1987) focused their work on juvenile sexual offenders. They suggest that when a male is victimized he is more likely to internalize guilt over his weakness and may express anger and powerlessness. Powerlessness can be turned into taking power over others and together with the anger could lead to sexual assault. All the aforementioned studies seem to suggest that the young people who have been sexually abused are already displaying signs of damage to child development by the time they reach puberty or adolescence.

Mediating factors on effects of abuse

In looking at the effects of sexual abuse on younger children, Lusk and Waterman (1986) also drew attention to the mediators which may contribute to the differential impact of the abuse. Existing problems in the family and the child's mental and emotional health prior to the abuse both seem to have an effect (Adams-Tucker 1981; Steele and Alexander 1981). There has also been speculation about the relationship of the child to the offender – most researchers agreeing that a closer relationship between offender and child means more resultant trauma (Adams-Tucker 1982; Steele and Alexander 1981).

There are conflicting results in studies which look at the relative maturity of the child at the time of first abuse. Some research indicates that younger children may suffer greater trauma (Adams-Tucker 1982; Steele and Alexander 1981), but other researchers have found that the effects are more damaging to older children (Schechter and Roberge 1976; Tsai *et al.* 1979). Younger children often display more physical symptoms (such as soiling) (see Cairns 1999, p.53) but older children who have been abused for a long time may have multiple problems which are not quite so obvious because their coping behaviours are better developed (Bannister 1997). Most studies agree that the abuse will affect children according to their age or developmental level (Dixen and Jenkins 1981).

More recent research makes it clear that long-term sexual abuse (which is likely to begin when the child is very young) is also frequently linked with emotional and physical abuse and victims are more likely to come from families who have existing problems (Bagley 1996). These children are, therefore, unlikely to have supportive carers who are able to alleviate some of the worst effects of abuse.

The nature of the abuse may also be a mediating factor in subsequent traumatic symptoms and it has been suggested that females suffer more trauma than do males. This may be because in the past males have tended to disclose abuse less often than females (Rogers and Terry 1984). However, recent revelations about large numbers of boys sexually abused in children's homes suggest that the problems eventually shown by these young men were the result of undiscovered, earlier sexual abuse (Doran and Brannan 1996). Most recent research suggests that the symptomology, post-abuse, is not gender specific (Briere *et al.* 1988).

Theories of child development

It has been observed by clinicians from Janet onwards that traumatized people tend to become fixated at the emotional and cognitive levels at which they were traumatized (van der Kolk 1996, p.204). Using knowledge of child development theories and tying these in with appropriate treatment options may go some way to solving these difficulties.

In Chapter One I set out some of the child development theories which had particularly influenced my colleagues and myself. These ecological and interactional theories of Moreno and Jennings/Slade may well have been influenced by earlier, similar theories by Bronfenbrenner (1979) and by Vygotsky (1934). More recently, Howe (1993) has stated that the brain is programmed with certain capacities but that its potential cannot be achieved until the environment provides examples and experiences for the potential state. Moreover, he states, the quality of the examples and the experiences will uniquely shape the eventual realization of the potential. Thus whatever the genetic inheritance (nature) of a particular child, the environmental experiences (nurture) will determine the shape of that child in the future.

Howe describes play with objects in children from 18 months and notes that these objects (toys, dolls) are endowed with mental states (projection). Howe remarks that most children, by the age of six, can begin to imagine the world from another's point of view. This capacity for role play and role reversal is an important ability for children. It helps them to play. Howe makes a comment (p.147) about therapy: 'If we are to gain new understandings of the meaning of our own experiences, we have to use the medium in which we originally learned to understand the meaning of those experiences.' He is talking here about the medium of language but, of course, the medium can be play, which may include language but also so much more. Howe describes art as 'the organisation of experience and the communication of meaning' (p.142). The creative therapies, which use all kinds of art, can help children (and adults) in finding meaning in chaotic and traumatic experiences which would have been incomprehensible to a child's mind.

If children are able to develop in a way which enables them to absorb experiences (or store them) until they are able to put meaning to them, it is more likely that they will reach their potential. Children who are bombarded with traumatic events which they cannot process may be unable to progress satisfactorily. It may be that they need to repeat some of their developmental processes, in creative play therapy, before they can integrate the traumatic events to which they have been subjected. It may also be possible that when a safe environment is established, where young people can retrace earlier development, then they can repeat some of those traumatic events (possibly in metaphor) and so understand their meaning.

The children then, with the support of the therapists, will be able to reorganize their lives to include their memories. This would prevent the intrusion of unwanted memories, would change states of amnesia, would raise self-esteem, and thus many of the symptoms of post-traumatic stress disorder would disappear.

Note

1   I checked through the records of approximately 50 women, i.e. all those referred to myself or my colleague over about four years because they had harmed their children, and made a note of whether they had declared that they had been abused. The resultant findings were discussed with my colleague, Prodgers, but were not written up. Because of confidentiality, the original records will not now be available for perusal.

CHAPTER THREE

Creative Therapies and Their Uses

Creativity and child development

Links with creative therapies and child development began for me when I was simultaneously training in psychodrama and dramatherapy and also working in an NSPCC centre where young mothers came with their infants to receive help with childcare. I watched the 'dance' between mother and child with fascination. Some of the women had been abusive or neglectful towards their children, but whatever the nature of the relationship, there was always a strong sense of the mutual importance of the interaction, even when it was hostile. Daniel Stern, that consummate 'baby watcher' (2002), in his new introduction to *The First Relationship*, first published in 1977, states: 'After so much observation of the micro-local level of mother–infant interaction, metaphors from music and dance not only crept into my writing but also became a way for me to think about what I saw. In a sense, the recognition of the pervasive existence and importance of temporal dynamics was born in this book' (p.13).

In my case, my creative arts background led me into using creative therapies and thus to recognize the similarities between this kind of therapy and the naturally occurring interactions between children and their caregivers. I was discovering the links between art and healing. The use of dance, song and ritual has been connected with healing throughout history, as has visual art, poetry and storytelling. Marina Warner (1994), writing her epic study of fairytales, states: 'I began investigating the meaning of the tales themselves, but I soon found that it was essential to look at the context in which they were told, at who was telling them to whom, and why' (p.xii). Fairytales are doubtless metaphors for many truths, but they can only be understood in context. Their deep significance in many cultures is clearly not confined to children.

In my own work I have used fairy stories, particularly the story of *Little Red Riding Hood*, in work with sexually abused children and adult women. I have also used the folk tale *The Lingworm* with a 12-year-old sexually abused boy (Bannister 1997, pp.87–90). More recently, in one of my research groups of 7–9-year-old children, they spontaneously used the story of *The Three Little Pigs* (see Chapter Six). The same story was used by a five-year-old boy whom I saw in individual therapy (Bannister 1997, pp.79–80). Dramatherapists such as Cattanach (1997) and Gersie (1992) have also documented their use of stories with children.

Warner reminds us of the multitude of fairy stories about children brought up with absent mothers, with 'wicked stepmothers' or 'wicked uncles'. Recognizing the relevance of fairy stories for abused children becomes obvious. The *Cinderella* story, for instance, which is known in many cultures in different disguises, epitomizes this, and is often chosen by abused children themselves in their enactments, both in play and in therapy (Bannister 1997, pp.80–81). Indeed, Warner devotes a section of her study to analysis of a fairy story known as *The Donkeyskin* which tells the tale of a father who wishes to marry his daughter. She states that this story was widely told in many cultures (probably first published in 1694 in France) but has since been suppressed. The connection with child sexual abuse is made overt in the story. For the 'happy ending', when the daughter marries her prince, the father comes to the wedding 'purified of his odieuse flamme' (odious passion) (p.324).

When such stories are acted out by children their bodies adopt the movements and posture of the fairytale characters. This enhances their understanding, which is not necessarily cognitive. When adults tell such stories to children it is often during moments of closeness, when attachments are being made or reinforced. The adult(s) and child (children) make connections, through the story, in 'the space between'. Neuro-scientists tell us that the right brain hemisphere is concerned with artistic pursuits, whereas the left brain hemisphere influences more cognitive experiences. It may be that creative therapies, working from the right brain, help to make physical connections in our bodies. The essential connection between our bodies and minds has been recognized by shamans in various cultures, in Chinese medicine and, more recently, in holistic treatments.

In the 20th century the re-emergence of such treatments has often been credited to J.L. Moreno, a psychiatrist living in Vienna during the 1920s (see Chapter One). He had been influenced by his older contemporary Freud, but Moreno described his own work as 'putting the humour back into psychiatry'. Marx also influenced him and Moreno intended his kind of psychiatry, which he named psychodrama, to include 'the whole of mankind'. It is interesting that he first discovered psychodrama by watching children playing in the public gardens of Vienna. The links with play and with children are extremely important in Moreno's work and his understanding of child development is crucial to his theory of spontaneity and how this influences healing (Moreno 1977; Moreno 1993; Blatner 1997; Karp, Holmes and Bradshaw-Tauvon 1998). Karp, who trained with Moreno, states that he also stressed the essential use of the body in therapy and often reminded his students, 'the body remembers what the mind forgets' (Karp, personal communication 1978).

Psychodrama

Psychodrama (literally 'mind action') is closely connected to theatre, although it is theatre without a script, where the actors act out scenes from their own lives. The director is also the therapist and conducts the action which is determined by the protagonist (or main actor), assisted by auxiliaries who may be trained therapists or may be other members of a therapeutic group. Moreno also discovered sociometry through his interest in the relationships between people in groups and so psychodrama became a psychotherapeutic method which was largely practised in groups. However, the method can be used in one-to-one sessions by using inanimate objects instead of people. This is where the similarities to play are most apparent as dolls and puppets, or even cushions and other objects, can be used to represent people, animals, buildings or simply ideas or concepts.

Psychodrama can be used in many applications, not only with children and adolescents. It is commonly used with adults who have been sexually abused, with those who are suffering from alcohol or drug dependency, with sexual abusers and with people suffering from terminal illness (see Holmes and Karp 1991 for examples of all these applications). It may also be combined with other therapies, as I have done with dramatherapy and play therapy, and with other psychological theories. Farmer (1998), a practising psychiatrist who is also a qualified psychodramatist, uses standard medication for his depressive patients to treat the brain malfunction, but then also uses psychodrama to treat the underlying psychological stress. Holmes (1992), who is also a psychiatrist, combines object relations theory and psychodrama in his practice, especially with adolescents. Psychodramatists then, like most arts therapists, receive influences from many sources.

Moreno's interest in child development has already been described in Chapter One. He stressed the three developmental stages of finding identity, recognizing the self, and recognizing the other. These stages, which are normally facilitated in the child by the mother or main carer, can be damaged or delayed by traumatic experiences (Herman 1992). Psychodrama uses the techniques of doubling, mirroring and role reversal to replicate those developmental stages and to allow healing or re-growth.

Research into psychodrama has proliferated during recent years. Since 1994 there have been more than 50 research papers published on the effects of psychodrama, several of them in Germany, where psychodrama is flourishing, and others published in the USA, India, Turkey, Spain, South America and the UK. Of particular relevance to my own research is a study by Carbonell and Parteleno-Barehmi (1999) describing psychodrama groups for girls coping with trauma, and several investigations by Hudgins (1998) and her colleagues (Hudgins and Drucker 1998; Hudgins, Drucker and Metcalf 2000), into psychodrama with sexual trauma. All appeared to show the effectiveness of psychodramatic interventions with their particular client group. Hudgins' work in the USA with women survivors of sexual abuse has many parallels with my own since she uses a concept which she calls the 'containing double'. This is closely related to the developmental technique of doubling in psychodrama, which is a key component of my work with children.

Other relevant research is by Mehdi, Sen and Sen (1997), which studies the effect of psychodrama with depressed patients, since depression is a common symptom amongst adult women who have been sexually abused. More specifically, Pearson (1994) worked with adult female survivors of childhood sexual abuse in the USA, using psychodrama effectively. Ragsdale et al. (1996) studied the effect of short-term inpatient treatment, using psychodrama and counselling with war-related PTSD patients, and specifically with children. Ruiz Lazaro, Velilla Picazo and Bonals Pi(1996) used psychodrama effectively with school children in a psychiatric unit. All these studies showed that psychodrama was a useful intervention.

Dramatherapy

Whilst psychodrama was already flourishing in the USA and parts of Europe from the 1940s, dramatherapy was developing in the UK around the same time. Peter Slade (1995) is often credited with the use of drama as therapy, which emerged from his work in education. He was deeply aware of the importance of children's play and the part it played in human development. Like Moreno he did not concentrate simply on therapeutic aspects of drama or of play, but more on their essential value in the nature of healthy growth. He understood the importance of rituals which children incorporate naturally into their play, and the value of fantasy. He stresses the importance of 'Personal Play', which he equates with action by the child (using the body). He then describes 'Projected Play', in which the child incorporates other objects such as toys or drawing materials, etc. He makes it clear that both Personal and Projected Play continues, and is still very necessary for development, up to early adolescence. Then he stresses the importance of role play and what he terms 'social drama'.

Dramatherapy was further developed by anthropologist Sue Jennings (1987). She describes a period in the early sixties in Britain when the application of drama within the educational framework began to direct itself towards work in clinical areas. Jennings' description of a dramatherapy theory of child development, derived from Slade, is quoted by me in Chapter One. Jennings (1995) also describes many applications of the method, in groups or with individuals, with children and adults, with psychiatric patients and with elderly people, etc.

Dramatherapy has attracted many practitioners with an interest in theatre and literature and so the method has been enriched by applications which use Shakespeare's plays, Greek myths and drama, and fairytales. It is often called 'therapeutic theatre'. Unlike psychodrama, dramatherapy does not usually have a single protagonist who overtly works through personal difficulties, within a group or one-to-one setting. A dramatherapy setting is most likely to be a group, which may have some homogeneity – for example, the group may consist of people with learning disabilities.

However, the personal work which is done by the participants is likely to be done through dramatic distancing and symbolic identification. As in psychodrama, the group may choose to work at a pre-verbal level and may well use archetypes. Like play therapy, described below, dramatherapy is also influenced by the Sesame method, pioneered by Marian Lindkvist (Pearson 1996), where the emphasis is purely on the body and is largely non-verbal.

Like psychodrama, dramatherapy has also been well researched in the UK. Much research has been carried out by Jennings, especially with regard to infertility, by Dokter, with regard to anthropological and cultural aspects, and by Grainger, especially with regard to religion and health. Details of this (mostly unpublished research) can be found in Payne's *Handbook of Inquiry in the Arts Therapies: One River, Many Currents* (1993). Of particular relevance to my own research is the work done by Winn (1994) on the use of dramatherapy in the treatment of post-traumatic stress disorder. Although her work was directed towards adults, such as servicemen, police and emergency personnel who had suffered PTSD, rather than children who had been abused, she demonstrated the effectiveness of dramatherapy in their recovery. She suggests that this is because dramatherapy acts directly upon the person's feelings. It does not depend upon verbal accounts of the traumatic incident which, she suggests, many professionals are adept at giving without engaging their emotions. For the same reason, children can benefit from dramatherapy because they may not have words to describe their experiences.

Play therapy

American psychologist Virginia Axline is responsible for the growth of play therapy, which she developed from her clinical work with individual children. She stated that 'there seems to be a powerful force within each individual which strives continuously for complete self realization' (Axline 1947). She related this to the acceptance of the self, by the self, and by others. She followed the Rogerian concept of unconditional positive regard (Rogers 1951) in her therapeutic work and she demonstrated her understanding of the developmental necessity for children to play. Through working in a non-directive way with children she was able to get in touch with their ability to heal themselves. By creating a safe, totally accepting environment for the child, with clear boundaries, she enabled children to be themselves, to understand their own identity and that of others. By express-ing emotions and having these validated and reflected back, children could truly develop their personalities and even overcome damage from trauma.

The work of the French child psychoanalyst Francoise Dolto[1] in Paris, during the second half of the 20th century, should not be overlooked. She worked often with very young children, together with their mother or other carer. In speaking directly to the child (and not to the adult about the child) she formed a way of working which she termed 'talking true'. She was aware also of her own intuitive sense, watching carefully for body and facial gestures from the child, and she was aware of a non-verbal intuitive exchange between herself and the child. It seems to me that she was working within the potential space, described by Winnicott, which I describe as 'the space between'. She also advocated the use of puppets in talking and playing with children and so could be described as an early play therapist. Dolto's work was original but therapeutic work with children, using puppets, was described even earlier (Bender and Woltman 1936, 1937). Bender and Woltman used 'puppet shows' with 'behavior problem children'. Later, Lyle and Holly (1941) described the therapeutic value of puppets and Woltman (1943) described his experiences of using puppets in a child guidance setting.

Play therapy has been further developed in the UK by, amongst others, West (1992) and by Wilson, Kendrick and Ryan (1992). West describes her work as 'child-centred'; this expression was also used by myself (Bannister 1990/1998) in a description of the interactive play therapy which was developed by a team of social workers and myself in 1987–88 (see Chapter One). The term 'child centred play therapy' was probably first used by Moustakas (1953). Wilson, Kendrick and Ryan have described their work as 'non-directive play therapy' and they follow a more Rogerian approach which, perhaps, has less connection with psychodrama or dramatherapy. Cattanach's model of play therapy (1992) recognizes the importance of the child's developmental process and emphasizes the symbolism of play. My own approach to play therapy has many similarities to Cattanach's model. It could be characterized by the following points:

- *Child centred*: always allowing the child to lead but valuing spontaneity and creativity and *interaction* between therapist(s) and child (children).

- *Developmentally aware*: recognizing the developmental processes which are taking place in each child, and understanding that play is a vehicle for growth.

- *Emphasizing safety*: especially by using symbolism and metaphor and by containment/boundaries.

- *Tending towards action and the use of the body*: as pioneered by Moreno in psychodrama.

Creative therapies, or arts therapies

Although creative therapists may have been trained as art therapists, music therapists or dance movement therapists, for example, many will use their creativity eclectically, but within the boundaries of their theoretical disciplines. My own theoretical training has been in psychodrama and dramatherapy but when working with children I have adapted these to include Axline's methods of play therapy, and have evolved the model shown above. Like Cattanach (1992), I have used dramatherapy techniques of fantasy and storytelling to enrich the play which the child brings. When play is interactive, between two or more people, each person brings their own spontaneity and creativity to it. This means that although children's needs and wishes are totally respected, they are enabled to extend their play if they wish, and to expand it so that they can realize their own potential.

Although I am not trained in art therapy or music therapy, children often wish to use art or music in therapy with me. Art materials are always provided therefore and each child will use these as they wish. I am a musician and singer, and am aware that frequently the use of the voice is important for children. Several children wish to increase the strength of their voice, in order to be heard, and I sometimes use singing exercises for this. One adolescent worked by means of dance and song, with the assistance of pop music tapes, which she supplied. Play therapy benefits from its eclecticism and doubtless uses many theories from music therapy and dance movement therapy. The therapeutic experience is in the creativity the child brings, however that is expressed, and in its acceptance and understanding by the therapist.

Rationale for the use of creative therapies with sexually abused children

It is clear from the literature that various treatment methods can be beneficial to sexually abused children. It is difficult to know whether these are effective in the long term as well as the short term. It is hard to judge the relative severity of abuse suffered by different children. Indeed I believe that such a measure is impossible because each child is so affected by the environment, by all the variables of the abuse itself, and by subsequent support, that 'treatment' or 'therapy' is only one small part of the equation. A child centred approach, which can take into account the differences between children, in their history and in their present circumstances, is obviously necessary. A flexible method, which does not contain a set plan or programme, appears to be more suitable.

It is vital, though, that such a method should be grounded in theory; otherwise any treatment may be merely palliative in the short term. It is possible that there is no treatment that can provide long-term benefits. A look at the literature on therapy with adults who have been sexually abused in childhood seems to indicate that many people have problems throughout their lives, probably as a result of their childhood trauma. However, treatment for sexually abused children was almost unknown 20 years ago and is still relatively rare.

I have suggested that children, from a very early age, can respond to therapeutic interventions which can help them to recover from the damage caused by child sexual abuse. Kazdin (1994) reviewed the broad field of research into psychotherapy with children and adolescents. The young people concerned suffered all kinds of behavioural and emotional difficulties. The therapies used in the various studies included psychoanalysis and psychodynamically oriented psychotherapy, non-directive and relationship treatment, play therapy, behaviour therapy, cognitive behavioural therapy, family therapy, and school and community based treatment. Kazdin acknowledged that many other therapies remain neglected in the research with children. His studies showed that most treatments produce 'beneficial results'. He points out, however, that most studies did not include long-term follow-up, and two that did (18 months after treatment) showed great improvement on measures of neuroticism, anti-social behaviour, and total symptom scores, although early results from these two studies were not promising. We cannot rule out the idea that children may just 'grow out of' certain symptoms and anti-social behaviours. In other words, it is possible that their developmental and maturational processes operate sufficiently well to discard certain behaviours or symptoms, in due course. It is also possible that the treatments received in these two studies had an effect upon the children's development which was sufficiently strong to enable them to change their behaviour, over time. However, the two therapeutic methods used in these two studies are described as 'group therapy' and 'behavioural modification', methods which are generally considered to be very different in application.

Group therapy is a wide ranging term. Moreno is credited with first using the term 'group psychotherapy' in which he stressed the importance of the therapeutic interventions from fellow group members, as opposed to the focus being on the group leader. Group psychotherapy with young people, especially adolescents, has largely concentrated upon 'action methods' or 'creative methods', although the term can include group analysis. Group therapy with adolescents, as opposed to adults, is popular because adolescence is a time when the peer group probably has the most influence upon its members.

Behavioural modification, on the other hand, concentrates upon the dysfunctional symptoms and can include a system of rewards for good behaviour or can include explanations of anti-social behaviour (as in the treatment often used with adult sexual offenders). It is certainly feasible that the group therapy did not show immediate results, that it needed time and maturation to be effective. We do not know what the behaviour was that was being changed by behavioural modification. For instance, these methods are sometimes used effectively with symptoms such as bedwetting. However, bedwetting can sometimes be a sign of distress in a traumatized child. This subsides as the child learns other coping behaviours.

Trauma and reparative treatment

It is helpful to look at studies which show the likely effects of trauma on child development and how these effects may be overcome with treatment which mimics aspects of child development in a positive, reparative way. One such study is that of Young (1992) who links severe sexual abuse and the problem of embodiment of the trauma. I have already discussed the fact that abused children feel that their bodily integrity has been breached; many feel that their bodies are 'disgusting' or 'damaged'. Many children in therapy express fantasies of a 'dead baby' (Bannister 1995, pp.174–177) or feel that part of their body died in infancy. Young points to the fact that many of the effects of child sexual abuse concern the body: dissociation, multiple personality disorder (now known as dissociated identity disorder, DID), the eating disorders, somatic disturbances, self-mutilation and suicide. Dissociation, of course, is often described as 'leaving the body' and most victims of severe sexual abuse will experience this repeatedly for many years after the abuse. DID is an extreme form of dissociation.

As I have noted in the discussion on child development, our primary experiences are sensory rather than verbal and it may be that early experiences of sexual abuse are retained in sensory memory and cannot be expressed verbally but only somatically. As Moreno expressed it: 'The body remembers what the mind forgets.' It is noticeable in clinical work that many abused children suffer from somatic complaints such as headaches, stomach pains, problems of incontinence or bowel problems. Work has been done on the latter by Dr G. Devroede in Canada (personal communication 1994), who has shown links between sexual abuse and constipation and other bowel problems in adult women. In addition, much work has been published on somatic and emotional reactions to sexual abuse (Rapkin *et al.* 1990; Reiter and Gambone 1989; Rimsza, Berg and Locke 1988; Toomey *et al.* 1993; Walker *et al.* 1988).

Writing about work with adolescents, dramatherapist Renee Emunah (1995) also stresses 'identity cohesion' and the opportunity to express different roles. She also discusses the ease with which dramatherapy sessions can move to psychodrama and vice versa. Adolescents may prefer to begin working, within dramatherapy, on a hypothetical abuse situation and move to a specific situation, from their own lives, in psychodrama. Thus the ability to be flexible within the creative therapies is important.

A similar approach is used by Peter Pitzele (1991), describing his psychodramatic groupwork with adolescents in an inpatient psychiatric setting. Some of these young people had been physically or sexually abused. All suffered from crippled self-esteem. He recognizes that the young people with whom he works have an impaired sense of self – indeed he describes their use of 'the mask' through which they present themselves. His psychodramatic work looks at the mask, which he recognizes as a role, and he enables the adolescents to explore their identities which lie behind the mask.

Anna Chesner is a psychodramatist who also works in 'playback theatre'. Playback theatre is described as a ritual form of improvised theatre created in the moment by a unique collaboration of audience and players (Chesner 2002). She describes the safety and containment of the use of 'the mirror' in playback, where the protagonist watches others performing his or her own life drama. She states that the containment is also provided by the ritual form and that healing rituals stress appropriate aesthetic distance.

Young reminds us of the symptoms of anorexia and bulimia which many abuse survivors suffer and also the problems of obesity which beset other abused children. Young quotes Briere (1984) to illustrate his experience of a very high incidence of young people who have self-mutilated or made suicide attempts. Young concludes that the topic of embodiment has great relevance for research concerning the assessment and treatment of sexual abuse. He comments that dramatherapy and dance/movement therapy both use embodiment and he also mentions other arts therapies such as poetry therapy and art therapy which include aspects of embodiment that may be particularly relevant for sexual abuse survivors.

Pearson (1996) has written about the Sesame method of therapy which uses safety and containment and allows participants to 'play'. She likens the drama and movement sessions to the 'potential space' discussed by Winnicott. I would agree that such therapy occupies this space, 'the space between' as I have termed it. The Sesame method uses 'body memories' and allows participants to 'discover themselves' or 'find their identity' (pp.7–16). Pearson refers especially to its use with sexually abused children (p.55).

Finally I refer to Kellermann and Hudgins (2000) and their extensive psychodramatic work with people who have suffered trauma, particularly those suffering from PTSD. Kellermann states: 'Images, emotions and rec-ollections that are too painful are pushed out of awareness, but remain hidden within the body like foreign substances with psychosomatic mani-festations' (p.25). He considers that 'spontaneity…is responsible for the equilibrium of the person' (p.26). As a psychodramatist who trained with Moreno he believes that the recovery of spontaneity may be regarded as the 'lietmotif' for psychodrama with people who suffer from PTSD. Moreno believed that spontaneity was demonstrated by every child during the birth process and that it was essential for development. Trauma can inhibit spon-taneity but Kellermann reminds us that psychodramatic enactments can 'enable the growth of spontaneity that may alleviate the psychological impact of trauma' (p.26).

Kellermann edits his book on *Psychodrama with Trauma Survivors* (2000) with Hudgins, who has formulated a specific method for working with sexually abused women. The therapeutic spiral model (TSM) uses 'contain-ment, expression, repair, and integration of unprocessed trauma material' (p.230). Although Hudgins works primarily with adults, her model of psy-chodrama with sexual abuse survivors adds weight to the argument that sexual abuse can interfere with a child's developmental process. She uses developmental techniques such as 'the containing double' and Hudgins' research with Drucker and Metcalf (2000) demonstrates well the efficacy of psychodrama with sexual abuse survivors.

It may be that all these therapeutic approaches are similar to my own early work (Bannister 1990, reprinted 1998) in which I described the inter-active approach which I was using with sexually abused young children (see Chapter One). I had devised a therapy which was a mixture of techniques from play therapy, psychodrama and dramatherapy and, with my colleagues, came up with a description – the interactive approach. This name was meant to illustrate the fact that children contributed significantly towards their own healing. It seemed to be effective with the many sexually abused children who were seen by the team of therapists, of which I was a part. The hypothesis was formed that the interactive approach may duplicate the developmental processes which occur during infancy and childhood. It was recognized, of course, that the development of attachment may be dysfunc-tional or absent where there has been no opportunity for interaction between mother or permanent carer/s and the child.

This duplication of the attachment process may occur to some extent in any therapeutic alliance. However, it is the unique combination of this bond, together with the use of the body, the use of symbolism and non-verbal communication (in 'the space between') and the specific use of psychodramatic developmental techniques, which combine to make the interactive approach particularly valuable in the work with traumatized children.

I contend that the creative therapies in general and especially those that include embodiment, such as psychodrama, dramatherapy and play therapy, are particularly useful and relevant for child sexual abuse survivors for three major reasons:

- Severe sexual abuse trauma in early childhood causes damage to developmental processes (especially attachment processes), which must be addressed through therapy that repeats some of those processes in a positive way.

- Because of the damage to the embodiment process which occurs during child sexual abuse, treatment must address these physical problems by using complementary therapy which uses the body.

- Children who present for therapy must be contained in a safe way, which is also familiar to them. They must not be re-traumatized by re-experiencing their memories of abuse. The use of metaphor and symbolism is common in children's play where they use it to express and to contain frightening or dangerous feelings. In other words, the therapist must be aware of and respect 'the space between'.

The above three points provide a rationale for the use of creative therapies with sexually abused children. These points are further expanded below.

Damage to developmental processes, including attachment

The study of psychological trauma has been extensively covered by Herman (1998). She presents much evidence to show how traumatic events become frozen memories (pp.33–50). She gives many examples which show that traumatic memories lack verbal narrative and context, and that they are encoded in the form of vivid sensations and images. A particularly strong piece of evidence which she quotes is from Terr (1988), who had documented the histories of 20 children who had experienced severe trauma in their first two and a half years of life. None could give any verbal description of the documented trauma. However, at around the age of five, 18 of them were able to re-enact these events in their play with uncanny accuracy. One child, for instance, denied any knowledge or memory of his sexual abuse by a babysitter during his first two and a half years. In his play, however, he re-enacted scenes which showed a pornographic movie made by the babysitter. This kind of experience has also been documented by Citron (in Bannister and Huntington 2002). She describes a four-year-old child who played out (in therapy) a scene of sexual abuse with her father (which had been partially witnessed by the mother). The child later denied all knowledge of this abuse or of the play. Dr Citron remarks that the child may have been dissociating throughout the abuse and the play.

I suggest that since these sensory and iconic memories can apparently only be accessed in a sensory and iconic way, such as that provided in play, or creative therapies which use play, then these methods should be used to help children who have been abused during their developmental years. Indeed, it is not only children who can be helped. Adults who have been abused in childhood can also be helped to make sense of feelings which they are unable to understand. Herman also quotes Janet (1919) who explains that normal memory is the 'action of telling a story'. He stated that a 'fixed idea of a happening' is not, therefore, a memory in the true sense because the person has been unable to incorporate it in a narrative. Herman gives an example of a First World War veteran who was a very good narrator of his life story but when he came to his specific experiences in the trenches he became stilted and could only speak in brief exclamations of rage and betrayal.

These examples may show that traumatic memories are encoded in sensory ways, even in adulthood. Winn (1994) describes her dramatherapy work with soldiers who are suffering from PTSD. She shows how some veterans do not wish to remember the horrors they have experienced, but at the same time they wish to banish intrusive nightmares and flashbacks. Within the containment of metaphor and through the gentle process of dramatherapy, they are able to remember their experiences in iconic fashion and to incorporate them into their life histories, so giving themselves some control.

Because traumatic memories are so extensive for many children who have been severely abused from infancy, it is often the case that years of childhood experiences are merely remembered as horrifying, inexplicable 'flashbacks' or as very brief interludes of happiness. This means that these children have no clear narrative concerning their past lives and they cannot know completely who they are or how they should relate to others. Cattanach (1992) gives examples of stories which children tell her during therapy, which appear to be pure fantasy but which can be clearly related to their lives, as they remember them. In a psychodrama session with myself a girl told the story of a dragon which came to her house and took away both parents, leaving her to look after her younger brothers and sisters. While her parents were away a monster came in and stabbed her repeatedly, threatening her with death if she told anyone. The dragon then brought her parents back again but she could not tell them about the monster. This girl had been sexually abused by her step-father whilst both parents were under the influence of drugs.

Although traumatic experiences can damage developmental processes, most children will have also had some positive experiences during their early lives. The interaction between adults and children forms the material from which a child builds her sense of self. These positive acts help the child to know what she feels, who she is and how she can relate to others. It can be seen, therefore, that neglect of a child can also be extremely traumatizing and damaging, just as much as abuse. The effect of being a prisoner, within the family, is that a young child cannot make more positive connections outside the home environment. There are many examples in my own work, and that of others, where children were being severely abused or neglected by their immediate families. Some of these children, however, had good, positive connections with another relative, neighbour, or friend, who managed to input sufficient 'good enough mothering' to enable that child to develop with the minimum of damage.

One such boy is 'Fintan' described in Bannister (1997). He was severely sexually abused by many members of his immediate family, from birth until he was able to tell someone at the age of nine. The abuse took place on alternate weekends when he was taken, along with other siblings and cousins, to a designated place by older relatives. All the children were systematically abused by the adults, including grandparents. However, his maternal grandmother was not involved in this, and had no knowledge of it. On the weekends when he was not taken to the designated place, he was taken to stay with this grandmother, along with his younger siblings.

During his therapy with myself it became clear that he had made a good attachment to his maternal grandmother. He was thus able to make an attachment to a foster carer and to myself in therapy. His sense of self was severely damaged and he dissociated very frequently. His school work suffered, although he was clearly an intelligent child. However, I was struck by his insight into his feelings. He declared that his sense of honour had been lost because he 'allowed' the abuse to happen to his younger siblings. He felt he should have protected them. I felt that this showed that he had some sense of his self and that it was likely that his 'good' grandmother had been able to give this to him. He did find that making relationships with other children and with many adults was difficult. It seemed to me that his grandmother, who had cared for him since birth, even though it was only on alternate weekends, had a powerful mitigating effect on the damage caused by the abuse.

All these examples from clinical work can now be endorsed by neurobiology. For instance, Schore (1994) sees that the attachment process plays a vital part in development and he endorses the work of Ainsworth (1969), who recognized that developmental psychology had to be integrated with biology if we were to understand child development fully. Schore states that face-to-face reciprocal gaze transactions between mother and child induce particular neuroendocrine changes which 'imprint' on the child's brain and cause 'high levels of positive affect and play behaviour, and subsequently the establishment of the capacity to form an interactive representational model that underlies an early functional system of affect regulation' (p.65). Schore also refers to object relations theory to endorse his comments on the importance of *emotional interactions* between the child and others around them.

Damage to the embodiment process

My second point concerns the importance of embodiment, or somatization, both in the abusive experience and in the kind of treatment offered. Van der Kolk *et al.* (1996) state that there can no longer be any clear demarcations between psychological and biological processes (p.65). They quote Kolb

(1987) who proposed that excessive stimulation of the nervous system at the time of trauma may result in permanent neurological changes. Kolb was an army psychiatrist who has studied the effects of World War Two on combat survivors. The authors go on to stress the almost inevitable use of dissociation, at the time of abuse. This 'splitting' of the body and mind is clearly a protective mechanism, but it may lead to bodily feelings and symptoms which remain 'split off' and cannot be integrated or explained in the usual ways. Van der Kolk (in van der Kolk *et al.* 1996, p.193) describes his own experiments on the brain, using PET (positron emission tomography) scan studies of people with PTSD. He comes to the conclusion that the 'speechless terror', which is suffered during intense trauma, leads to an inability to put feelings into words, leaving emotions to be mutely expressed by bodily dysfunction. How much more likely is this effect when young children with limited speech suffer such trauma?

As already discussed, some bodily dysfunctions which are common in sufferers of PTSD are eating disorders such as anorexia and bulimia. Even more common are problems of obesity and of body image. Chronic muscle tension is another symptom described by Briere and Runtz (1988) in a large and long-scale study of women who were sexually abused in childhood. Numbness in certain parts of the body is mentioned by Lindberg and Distad (1985) in another study of such women. Not knowing what one feels, or being unable to put feelings into words, is a symptom almost universally described in my own professional experience. Only the tensions or other reactions of the body give a true indication of feelings about the abuse.

Such overwhelming data seem to support the otherwise surprising conclusions of van der Kolk *et al.* (1993) and of Saxe *et al.* (1994) (following extensive field trials), that such somatization rarely occurs except in those with a history of trauma. Van der Kolk (1996), describing his study with women who dissociate, states: 'Prone to action and deficient in words these patients can often express their internal states more articulately in movements or pictures than in words. *Utilising drawings and psychodrama* may help them develop a language that is essential for effective communication and for the symbolic transformation that can occur in psychotherapy' (p.195, my italics).

Sanderson (1995) extols the benefits of experiential therapies such as art, dance movement, dramatherapy and psychodrama with adult survivors of child sexual abuse. However, she recognizes the power of such therapies and suggests caution before they are introduced. She also includes body massage in her list of powerful therapies which can help with the somatic symptoms. I comply with her caution and agree that these therapies should not be tried with sexual abuse survivors by those who are not well qualified and experienced and who do not understand their cathartic effects.

Safe containment, the use of metaphor and 'the space between'

It is probable that 'the space between' (Winnicott's 'potential space') is the same notion which was proposed by Vygotsky as 'the zone of proximal development' (ZPD). Newman and Holzman (1993) state that this 'space' is actually an activity wherein learning takes place. Vygotsky declared the ZPD to be 'the relationship between people'. He was a psychologist who was concerned with how children learn and his discoveries were based on practice. For him learning and development were inseparable and he stressed the importance of metaphor which could be accepted, rather than interpreted.

The containing effects of metaphor, as experienced in art, dance movement, play and dramatherapy (and to some extent, psychodrama), are an essential part of the therapeutic effects with all those people who are suffering from PTSD. In addition, for those who work with children, an understanding of child development will assist the practitioner in introducing therapeutic techniques at a level which the child can tolerate. It is important that the child centred, interactive approach is maintained when working with metaphor. It is always preferable to use the metaphor which a child uses spontaneously, rather than to introduce one which may have meaning for the adult therapist. In therapeutic work with children there are a number of books which contain selections of stories which retell abusive incidents in an imaginative way. The heroes and heroines in the story succeed because they manage to overcome the villains by accepting help and by realizing their own potential. Often the fairytale format is used and frequently the characters in the story are animals or mythical creatures. However, I suggest that these stories should be used with discretion since they can only have real meaning if a child happens to relate to the metaphor.

In *The Healing Drama* (1997) I quoted a case study of my own in which a boy had drawn a butterfly and a chrysalis and had stated that he wanted to change from the chrysalis, whom no one could reach, to the butterfly who could spread his wings and fly. I was able to take that metaphor of transformation to tell him the ancient folk tale of *The Lingworm* who had to shed his skins in order to become human again. The boy immediately adopted the metaphor and during sessions he metaphorically removed layers of protective, but potentially damaging coping mechanisms, within the safety of the therapeutic containment. Eventually he was able to 'spread his wings' and fly.

In the pilot of the clinical group for my recent research, the children spontaneously introduced the story of *The Three Little Pigs*. The theme behind this story is that the three little pigs were, at first, not able to protect themselves from the wolf. Eventually, however, they learned how to build a strong house of bricks which protected them and in addition they managed to destroy the wolf. The children at first modelled small pigs from clay, and built fences to protect them from the wolf. They played 'wolf and sheep' catching games and tried to keep themselves safe from harm. The therapists to the group used this metaphor, which the children had presented, and helped them to develop a group story in which they became 'little pigs' who could support each other. The original fairytale was changed by the children so that the 'mother pig' was seduced by the 'wolf'. She invited him into their house which he built more strongly but *with himself inside this stronghold*. Eventually, the children were able to tell their mother of the danger and she realized her error, and was able to support the 'little pigs' who banished the wolf from their house (see Chapter Six for more information on the use of this story).

I believe that the children were only able to use this metaphor so successfully because they had gained some insight, during the group, and realized that they were not to blame for their own abuse. They were, however, blaming their mothers who had allowed the abuser into their home. They had not realized that their mothers may also be victims. Because they used the story metaphor spontaneously and frequently, it was fruitful for the therapists to suggest continuing this story. At the end of the group they acted out the story with great enthusiasm and an obvious sense of achievement. It is doubtful if this could have been achieved so successfully if the therapists had used the original story and adapted it without reference to the children's own sense of meaning.

Recognition of, and sensitivity to, 'the space between' child or children and therapist(s) ensures that therapists will not be intrusive or prescriptive. It respects and nurtures children's innate creativity and their ability for self healing. It recognizes the necessity for interaction on many levels and understands that children's metaphors may not always be fully understood by adults (who may have forgotten some of their own reference points). Indeed, therapists with very different backgrounds from their abused child clients may not always understand the symbolism and metaphor which those children use. This does not invalidate the children's experience. It is sometimes the case that therapists realize retrospectively, often in their own supervision sessions, exactly how children have been working with them in therapy on their abusive experiences.

Conclusion

It seems to me that being treated as a whole person, instead of a collection of symptoms or behaviours, is a respectful way for a therapist to interact with another person. Howe (1993) states that in therapy it is not the specific technique which is important but the manner in which it is done and the way it is experienced (p.3). He discusses the empathy which, it is generally agreed, is necessary for successful communication in therapy. Empathy corresponds to some degree with 'tele' as described by Moreno. Howe looks in detail at how empathy works, how one person might be able to understand the thoughts and feelings of another. His first explanation is metaphysical; it is a belief that human beings have a deep-seated ability to commune directly with the experience of each other. This explanation would meet much of the criteria for the tele which Moreno describes. Second, Howe states that the second explanation of empathy is based on the quality of our physical perceptions of the world around us, particularly the world of people; empathy depends on acute and sensitive observation. Last, Howe suggests a sociological explanation, recognizing that the self emerges out of and develops within a shared social world.

Howe agrees, of course, that a combination of all these aspects is present in most therapists with empathy. I suggest that successful empathy with children and young people includes all the above factors, but includes another factor or factors which may depend on the ability of the therapist to be in touch with his or her own inner child. This in turn may relate to the amount of spontaneity and creativity which a therapist has and it may also relate to the extent to which a therapist allows himself/herself to be vulnerable. I suggest that these personal qualities may be more apparent in someone who has trained in a method of therapy where play and fantasy are used as a matter of course, where training is usually focused in peer groups, and where vulnerability is valued and shared. This describes the training for most kinds of creative therapies.

However, Dr Stephen Prior (1996), speaking from a psychodynamic perspective regarding psychotherapy with a sexually abused child, also demonstrates his empathy as he describes how he engages with a child in a way which I would consider to be not dissimilar to that of a creative therapist. The example he uses is of a boy who states his belief that 'Dr Prior is going to hump me...' Prior immediately 'doubles' the child, stating the feeling: '*How scary it would be* if you thought I was really going to do that.' Prior describes the boy's statement (in psychoanalytic terms) as a 'transferential fear' and it is after this that the boy is able to talk about his horrific abuse. Dr Prior also allows the boy to express very violent play, as a play therapist would, and states that the presence of the violent play is a sign of the therapeutic alliance.

Some therapists, including creative therapists, have expressed doubts about allowing a child to express violent play because it may either re-traumatize the child or may allow him to feel justified in behaving violently in other, inappropriate settings. Prior states that, in fact, the child may be re-traumatized if he is *not* allowed to convey the reality of his experience in the only way he knows how. I agree with him in that the child should be allowed to do this, but should be contained in a safe way so that he is not allowed to harm himself or others, or damage equipment. Prior lists four essential ways of responding to such a child as:

1. The sharing of experience (which I would expand into 'doubling').

2. Labelling and naming experiences (which I would label 'mirroring').

3. Understanding the wish to be identified with an aggressor (which I would call 'role playing coping behaviours').

4.   Allowing the child to find underlying relational needs (which I would demonstrate with 'role reversals').

It may well be, therefore, that some of the aspects of creative therapy are used in other 'talking therapies' but, nevertheless, it is the holistic nature of creative therapies which are more likely to encompass all the aspects necessary for the healing of a child to take place. It is also important that the child feels that he or she has been enabled to heal, that 'I have done it myself' rather than 'the therapist has cured me'. Otherwise, the feelings of powerlessness may not be changed.

Note

1 I am indebted to Prof Anne Ancelin Schutzenberger for the information regarding Dr Dolto.

CHAPTER FOUR

Why are Children so Vulnerable?

Children in society

A social constructionist view of society suggests that 'identity arises out of interaction with other people and is based on language' (Burr 1995, p.51). Burr goes on to suggest that our identity is defined by our social discourses. I would add that language may play only a small part in our identities (especially in childhood) and that much more may be learned by observation and example. For instance, we now have evidence that many children are strongly affected by domestic violence that they witness in their homes (Skuse *et al.* 1998). This study shows that boys who have been sexually abused, and who have also witnessed 'intrafamilial violence', are more likely to sexually abuse other children when they are adolescents.

Most children who are sexually abused do not sexually abuse others. If they did, the majority of abusers would be female since, as far as we know at present, more girls are sexually abused than boys (Bolen, Russell and Scannapieco in Itzin 2000). Although some women do sexually abuse, the overwhelming evidence is that there are more males who are sexual abusers. It would seem then that boys, in particular, become conditioned towards violent and controlling behaviour if they have experienced or witnessed such behaviour from adult males in their close environment (Finkelhor 1994). Sexually abusive behaviour is, like physical abuse, a violent form of control and some boys may, as soon as they reach adolescence or even before, attempt to control others in this way. Such behaviour may lead to the so-called 'cycle of abuse' (Ryan and Lane 1991). Ryan makes the point that since most child sexual abuse is undiscovered, it may be that adults who were not helped when they were children may feel little empathy for children whom they subsequently abuse.

Children learn very quickly that sexual matters are seldom discussed in public, except perhaps with one's peer group. Because children have no yardstick with which to measure behaviour, they may believe that sexually abusive behaviour is normal. More than one early adolescent girl has told me that until puberty they assumed that all fathers behaved in a sexual manner towards their daughters. The abusing fathers also told them that this was private and should not be discussed. Often the fathers explained this by saying it was a way to teach girls about sex. Other abused children, more often boys, have stated that they were afraid of the reaction of their peers, if they told anyone. As boys reach puberty and learn about homosexuality they also fear that their peer group would think that they were gay. These fears are not misplaced since many children who do manage to tell, or whose abuse is discovered by adults, suffer bullying and ridicule from their peers.

Most theories of child development, including that of Moreno which I introduced earlier, suggest that children begin to understand that they have a separate identity during the early attachment process. Often an infant's first word will be 'No!' as she demonstrates clearly that her own needs are different from those of her mother. The next stage of development, however, that of 'role reversal' or 'understanding the other', increases gradually during infancy. By the age of four or five the child has learned to co-operate to a certain extent, to 'put herself in the shoes of another'. Her natural hedonism is more restrained as she understands that other people have needs also.

This desirable state, of course, can only be achieved if the child is capable of responding in the first place. Some children may have autistic tendencies which prevent them from fully understanding the world around them. Other children may be aware, but their main carers or attachment figures may have failed to help the children to regulate their emotions and responses. Their attachments may then be dysfunctional so that the children have an ambivalent or avoidant response to their caregivers. In some cases, especially if parents are abusive, the children may have a disorganized pattern of attachment where caregivers are seen as frightening or frightened and themselves as helpless, angry or unworthy. This leads to difficulties in being able, fully, to conceptualize other relationships in a different way.

As I worked with sexual offenders, I felt that this lack of awareness of the feelings of 'the other' was strikingly obvious. Some of these men believed that a naked child was 'provocative', and that a child's natural curiosity indicated sexual desire. They were only able to project their own feelings upon the child. The children who were abused told me of their loud protests as they were assaulted by the pain of abuse. 'They didn't seem to hear,' said one boy who was abused by several men. 'They said it didn't hurt really.' It may be that such offenders are unable to make close relationships in which they can understand the needs of another person. If that is so, it is likely that this inability stems from their own dysfunctional attachments in childhood.

Children with post-traumatic stress disorder

Children are still at a disadvantage in most societies. Their testimony is considered to be suspect, although there is no evidence to show that a child's recollection of an event is less reliable than that of an adult. People who have suffered traumatic events, however, especially if these have taken place over a period of time, may remember the events as a series of 'pictures', rather than as a narrative. As I have mentioned, this phenomenon has been known for some time, amongst practitioners working with veterans of the Second World War, and of the Vietnam conflict. The soldiers were eventually diagnosed with post-traumatic stress disorder (PTSD) but the similarities amongst children who had also suffered trauma were not recognized until more recently.

Briere and Runtz (1988) showed that the most common behavioural problems in children who have been sexually abused fit in with a diagnosis of PTSD. An update of the criteria for this diagnosis now includes particular references to children (American Psychiatric Association 1994). However, during the 1970s and 1980s there were publications (e.g. cited in Briere and Runtz 1988; Constantine 1980; Ramey 1979) suggesting that sexual contact between adults and children was not necessarily harmful. The acceptance of this view may be as a result of the 'accommodation syndrome' (Summit 1983) which I mentioned earlier. It means that children will be unlikely to tell of their abuse, and also that adults who have been abused may declare that they were not damaged by it.

Table 4.1 Complex post-traumatic stress disorder in children

A history of subjection to totalitarian systems in domestic life including childhood sexual abuse.

Alterations in consciousness including:

- Amnesia for traumatic events
- Transient dissociative episodes (often noticed in school)
- Reliving experiences (with children this is usually in play)

Alterations to coping mechanisms including:

- Suicidal preoccupation (even in children as young as six)
- Self-injury (in young children this can include scratching the skin until it bleeds)
- Explosive or extremely inhibited anger (these may alternate)

Alterations in self-perception including:

- Sense of helplessness (in children this may be hopelessness)
- Shame, guilt and self-blame
- Sense of defilement or stigma
- Sense of complete difference from others

Alterations in perception of perpetrator(s) including:

- Pre-occupation with relationship with perpetrator
- Unrealistic attribution of total power to perpetrator (in children this is often underlined when powerful adults fail to believe them)
- Idealization or paradoxical gratitude (if the perpetrator is also the main carer for a child this idealization is common)
- Sense of special or supernatural relationship (children are often told by their perpetrator that he/she can 'see everything')
- Acceptance of belief systems/rationalizations

Alterations in relationships with others including:

- Isolation and withdrawal
- Repeated search for rescuer (in children this is frequently shown in play)
- Persistent distrust
- Repeated failures of self-protection
- Over-controlling behaviour

Adapted from Herman (1998)

Herman (1992) has made a particular study of post-traumatic stress disorder in children who have been sexually abused. She points out that children who are survivors of prolonged, repeated trauma suffer from a variant of PTSD which she names complex PTSD. This includes a spectrum of symptoms which is far ranging. She notes the similarities in symptoms of people who have suffered other kinds of prolonged trauma such as survivors from the Nazi holocaust or refugees from oppressive regimes. She quotes many professionals who have also observed this wide spectrum of symptoms. I have adapted her broad classification to one which is specific to children who have suffered from prolonged physical and/or sexual abuse in early childhood, by abusers who are intimately involved in their victim's family life (see Table 4.1).

It will be seen from this list of symptoms that children who are suffering from complex post-traumatic stress disorder become even more vulnerable, within their immediate abusive situation and also within society. For instance, they may suffer amnesia for their most traumatic events. These may not be recalled until many years later, and sometimes even then only in flashbacks which do not fit into a continuous narrative. Such children may have transient dissociative episodes in school. If noticed at all, these episodes may be described as 'dreaming' and the child may be punished or ignored. Learning, of course, will be impossible during these episodes. The child could be considered to be 'odd' by other children or teachers and may become the butt of ridicule.

Other symptoms of complex PTSD which pose further dangers to the child are suicidal preoccupations, self-injury, or explosive anger. I was once asked to see a six-year-old girl who had leg injuries caused by a collison with a bus. The mother told me that she was holding the child's hand when she appeared deliberately to throw herself in front of the approaching vehicle. While the child was still in hospital she drew pictures with me. She drew herself in black, in her house, looking out at 'a black witch in a black hole' in the garden. She said the black witch was lonely and frightened. This was the first in a series of pictures that she drew with me. Her mother was already considering separation from her physically abusive husband. She told me that her husband called the child 'a witch'. The little girl soon began to describe her father's sexual abuse which may have been going on for some years.

This girl also suffered extreme shame, guilt and self-blame, exacerbated by the fact that her father constantly told her that what was happening was her own fault because her 'witch-like' behaviour was so provocative. She also drew herself with a 'black hole' between her legs and continually defined herself in her father's terms. It will be seen that her risk of suffering further abuse, even when she was removed from her father, was high because of her self-image and her inflated idea of her father's power.

It was never absolutely clear whether this child had tried to throw herself under the vehicle. She never brought up the subject in therapy and it is possible that her mother, who was also living with her own trauma, may have misread the child's actions or projected her own feelings onto the child. However, this child was also damaging herself by nibbling her nails down to the flesh and her teachers had noticed that she sometimes banged her head continuously against a wall. She had been living with physical and sexual abuse for as long as she could remember and she had accommodated to it sufficiently to keep it hidden for several years. It is this combination of suffering the effects of complex PTSD, and the accommodation syndrome, which further increases the vulnerability of an abused child.

It is interesting to consider the situation of children in societies where there are different cultures. Despite the fact that Article 19 of the UN Convention on the Rights of the Child states that children should be protected from all forms of physical or mental abuse, children in the UK are not afforded the protection from physical abuse which adults are. Adults who physically abuse other adults can be charged with assault. Physical abuse against children by parents and carers, including childminders, is tolerated, although the damage to the developing child may be considerably greater than the damage suffered by an adult. It is some years since physical assault in schools was condemned; that protection should be afforded to all children, even when they are within their own homes.

Itzin (2000) has pointed out that much of the huge volume of literature on child sexual abuse does nothing to either prevent its recurrence or to alleviate the sufferings of those who have been abused. I hope that this book may contribute to alleviating some suffering, and by giving children a voice (through creative therapy) it may also prevent some recurrence. To 'stop abusers abusing', however, means a radical change in society's attitudes to children.

Children in families

Children have little power within families and those who are abused are often held captive as effectively as if they had been imprisoned. Herman (1992) declares this to be as a result of their dependency and it is true that many children who succeed in 'running away' end up being dependent on others who exploit them. Just as women who are being abused by their partners have found it difficult to escape because of economic and psychological reasons, so children may find that there is 'nowhere to run'. Of course, physical restraint and violence can also provide effective deterrents to both women and children. There is still some reticence amongst 'officials' to intrude upon families where abuse may be occurring.

Constructs of childhood are intrinsically bound up with constructs of women. As Eichenbaum and Orbach (1982) pointed out: 'The present psychic structure of women derives from current child-rearing arrangements in which women bring up children in a patriarchal society' (p.98). Child-rearing arrangements have changed in the two decades since this was published and there is more awareness of the importance of fathers. In addition, the voices of women are now heard more often in positions of power. There is still some way to go, however, with regard to the voices of children.

Child protection systems are themselves subject to the views of childhood which society has at any given time. As Parton and Wattam (1999) point out, sexual abuse is treated differently from other forms of abuse, and intrusive investigative responses have not necessarily been child centred. Few children wish to have their lives disrupted in the way that often happens when sexual abuse is brought into the child protection system. One of the difficulties may lie in the way we communicate with children.

Communicating with children

Most of us recognize people who seem to communicate well with children. They automatically bring themselves to the same level as the child, they use their hands and faces expressively but never patronize or talk down to a child. They are creative and appear to be able to inspire creativity in children. They have 'a gift'. If they are professionals working with children, it is more likely that they have studied the various ways in which children communicate and have tried to expand their own communication skills.

In early attachment relationships children and their caregivers respond to each other without words. During the intense 'gaze' the child looks at the carer's eyes and neurobiological studies have shown how important this is in the bonding process (Panksepp, Siviy and Normansell 1985). As I have stated, Schore (1994) suggests that during this process the infant's maturing right hemisphere of the brain is psychobiologically attuned to the output of the mother's right hemisphere. It is also the case that in psychotherapy a similar bond – 'the therapeutic relationship' – can occur. This would appear to be confirmed by clinical studies (Langer 1992; Leichtman 1992) which show the clinical effectiveness of psychotherapy with brain-damaged children and adults. A study by Bach-y-Rita (1990) cited in Schore (1994) also confirms that the brain retains plasticity into adulthood so that this gives hope for those who have suffered brain injury or early psychological damage.

When adults communicate with children, therefore, we need to be aware of the non-verbal level of communication. This is most easily expressed in joint creativity. Play is the way that children express their creativity naturally and adults who are in touch with their own need to play may react spontaneously when a child initiates play. On the other hand, children whose playful behaviour has been discouraged or punished may need some encouragement from an adult or another child before they can relax into play. It is important not to use adult power in such a situation (showing the child how to 'do it right'), but to follow the child's lead and introduce one's own creativity gradually. Often playing in this way may leave adults feeling vulnerable as they temporarily lose some of their own coping behaviours. In a professional situation we need to be aware and accepting of our own vulnerability, without placing responsibility on the child.

As I have suggested in the previous chapter, those who work professionally to communicate with children, especially with abused children, may find that some knowledge of the creative therapies is important to assist them in communication. They are a more equal and joint way of communication so the young person is less likely to be intimidated by the inevitable power in an adult–child dyad. They are a safe and natural way of expressing feelings and of allowing the feelings to be witnessed. Creative therapies work safely in 'the space between' and help to reduce the vulnerability of children.

Children in schools

Some children who are being abused find that school is the only possible place for them to talk about what is happening. A fairly common scenario is that a child speaks first to a school friend, and the friend either tells a parent or teacher, or the friend encourages the abused child to tell the teacher. However, there are still many children for whom this would be impossible. Children who are being abused often have few close friends, sometimes because abusing parents have encouraged their isolation for their own reasons, or because the children feel 'different' and realize that their own experiences are not shared by their contemporaries.

Some teachers, of course, do recognize an under-achieving child who may have problems at home, and will do their utmost to befriend and support the child. Sexual abuse seldom leaves visible bruises or scars, however, and so it is not surprising that teachers in this situation have difficulties in intervening. Some children (and adults abused as children) have said that school was their refuge, the only place where they could feel safe. These are often the 'high achievers' who concentrate on academic work and avoid socializing (which could lead to embarrassing disclosures). Sometimes, in adolescence or later, these survivors of abuse find the family secrets too difficult to bear and may be diagnosed with 'borderline personality disorder' or 'depression'. We know that sexual abuse in childhood is a contributing factor to mental illness in women. There have been many studies of this – for instance, Briere and Runtz (1988) and Bifulco, Brown and Harris (1994).

Schools may, of course, also be places where further abuse occurs. For some children, especially those in foster homes, school is the place where their contemporaries bully and tease them about their home situations, or about their lack of achievement in the classroom. They are vulnerable simply because they are already victims. Of course, the children who are bullying may also be living in difficult or abusing home circumstances where their best coping behaviour seems to be 'over-control'. Some schools are excellent in spotting this behaviour and teachers and children work together to reduce it. Other children suffer within the school throughout their childhoods.

Children in therapy

The vulnerability of the adult is eclipsed by the vulnerability of a child in the therapy situation. The kind of communication with children which I described earlier is the opposite of the 'grooming behaviour' of abusers who impose their own needs upon children. They use their power to initiate behaviours in children which are gratifying to adults, whilst persuading the children that they too are benefiting from the behaviours. This is reminiscent of the phrase sometimes used by physical abusers who beat children as punishment: 'This is hurting me more than it hurts you!' However, professionals who are seeing children in a one-to-one setting must be aware that this situation may be reminiscent to the child of their former abuse. They should not assume that the child knows that they can be trusted and should be prepared to spend time building that trust and allowing the child as much control as possible.

Some adults who have been abused as children have expressed to me the wish that they had received therapy during their childhood. They have felt that this may have prevented some of the subsequent difficulties in their lives. Some of them have spent years in therapy as adults and know that healing takes time. It seems to me to be important that children who have suffered trauma receive support and assistance as soon as possible. Most of us, including children, respond to trauma by initiating our own coping behaviours. These can be extremely successful at the time and they enable us to continue functioning in unfavourable circumstances.

Such behaviours, however, may cause further problems for children and young people. If children are enduring repetitive and constant abuse they may find that the best way to cope is to acquiesce quietly and not to draw attention to themselves. Some children, especially girls, may see other females (perhaps their mothers) behaving in this way. Sometimes they may be told specifically (by non-abusing parents) that this is the safest way to behave. This attitude may also mean that the children do not tell anyone outside the family (or even within the family) of their experiences. They suffer in silence. Such children are sometimes difficult to engage in therapy because they wait patiently for the therapist to make the first move and they constantly try to please.

These are the 'watchful' children who are always on the alert for controlling, abusive behaviour in others. They comply with all suggestions and they find it difficult to initiate play. Most children are curious, however, and if the therapist is patient, the child will slowly respond and may eventually take the initiative once trust is established. It is important that the child's way of coping is not denounced. One junior school girl said in therapy, 'They don't do it if you shout and tell, do they?' She was referring to a 'lesson' which the whole class had received, where children were advised to 'Shout and Tell!' if a paedophile tried to abuse them.

This child had been abused for many years by her father and she had coped by being silent and obedient. Since most abused children feel that they must be at fault to have attracted such behaviour, she felt later on that her way of coping was the reason that she had been abused. It was helpful for her when the therapist empathized with her situation. Later, praise for initiative and self-affirming behaviour would be in order so that she could then decide when it was appropriate to discard her original coping behaviour which had become dysfunctional.

Similarly children, often boys, who present with very aggressive behaviour, need to be contained and supported. Their aggressive behaviour may have felt like a good way to cope with the aggression of an adult so it is helpful if it can be channelled safely in therapy. Diverting aggression from self-destruction or the destruction of toys within the room may be crucial in forming a therapeutic alliance with a child. Their 'righteous' anger about their abuse can be confirmed by a therapist who 'doubles' for the child, standing alongside and repeating angry behaviour in a safe way (such as hitting cushions with rolled-up newspapers). Once this rapport is made the child usually finds that it is not necessary to repeat the behaviour. Simply forbidding or discouraging the expression of anger in therapy is more likely to encourage its use at school or elsewhere. Clearly, too, a boy who is using very controlling behaviour, albeit as a coping mechanism, is more likely to become a physical or sexual abuser of others.

I have suggested that a child who is dissociating in therapy should be accommodated as far as possible and accepted. As I documented in the last chapter, children frequently dissociate during their abuse. It is another useful coping mechanism. This means that in addition to the fact that early memories are iconic rather than narrative, children's memories of abuse may be further damaged because of dissociation. Sometimes in therapy abused children seem to 'flip out' or to gaze into space, occasionally they may behave in uncharacteristic ways for a few moments, before returning to their usual mode. At such times they may not respond to the therapist. Accepting this behaviour is important for the relationship, but if it recurs it may be important to note what behaviour in the therapist may have triggered it. I have noticed that this usually disappears when a good relationship has been established, although teachers sometimes report that it persists in the classroom.

Successful therapy with children depends, of course, on the child's home situation. This is part of the initial assessment and is vital to a successful outcome. Naturally, children must feel safe before they can begin the therapeutic journey so caregivers must provide that safety in a positive way. Separate individual therapy with parents may be necessary or a supportive group may be more suitable. Sometimes non-abusing parents (and foster parents) simply need to have child therapy explained and to understand that behaviour will not necessarily change immediately. Sometimes behavioural changes are unwelcome, such as when a passive, silent child becomes assertive and noisy. Caregivers may need a good deal of support with these changes.

My recent research appears to confirm that having supportive caregivers for children in therapy is not only desirable, but essential. A retrospective case study of a young person with whom I had worked together some eight years previously revealed this to be true. At the time this 12-year-old girl was in a foster placement where she had been since her removal from a neglecting and abusive home situation some two years previously. Her behaviour at home was deteriorating and she was referred for therapy. However, the foster parents' response to therapy seemed inappropriate and the girl herself was asking for a new foster placement. The social worker and I both agreed that a new placement was needed but naturally this took some time to arrange. Administrative difficulties meant that the girl could not then continue her therapy with me. In discussion some 12 years later she confirmed that the therapy had been effectively sabotaged and denigrated by the first foster parents.

Some interesting therapeutic work is now being carried out with foster and adoptive parents, and the children who have previously been abused. It is recognized that new attachments must be made between the children and the new caregivers. In addition, creative work is being done to help the children to 'piece together' their iconic memories and to make a narrative which children and caregivers can share. This kind of joint work with therapist(s), social workers, caregivers and children is a good example of shared creativity, working in a playful way, in the space between. For good examples of this work see Chapters 11 and 12, by Paul Holmes and Chip Chimera respectively, in Bannister and Huntington (2002). Chimera acknowledges that, although this therapy may be essential to assist children and their new carers to form new attachments, further individual work may be needed with the children. Since both caregivers and children appear to respond so well to creative therapy in these projects, it seems sensible to continue working with creative therapies in any individual work with the children.

For children from around the age of seven and upwards, therapy in peer groups may be the most useful intervention. However, group therapy with younger children may also be effective, as quoted in Chapter Six of this volume. In my recent research, group therapy was the method adopted, and the details will be discussed later in this book. Some children benefit from the fact that they are able to meet other children who have been abused. They may have felt isolated and alone until they discovered that their experiences were not unique. There may be some vulnerability also in the group experience. Some children who are still feeling guilty may not wish anyone other than the therapist to know of their experiences. However, these same children, if they can overcome their early doubts, may be the ones who benefit the most. They will empathize strongly with other children and recognize the vulnerability of such children before, eventually, recognizing and accepting their own.

Conclusions

The vulnerability of children to abuse may be summed up by the fact that child abuse is always an abuse of power and children remain powerless in most situations: in society, in the family and in school. Children often lack a voice, and adults may not know how to communicate with them. To empower children, to give them a voice, must be our aim. Those who work with children with disabilities, i.e. children who suffer prejudice and discrimination because of perceived functional difficulties, know how difficult it is for such children to have a voice in society. This prejudice continues for many during their adult lives also. If they have learning difficulties the prejudice and discrimination may be compounded by the ignorance and fear of some adults and institutions.

Children, of course, grow up and for some abused children this provides an opportunity to speak out on behalf of others who are abused. But for others, abuse in childhood always remains an unspoken secret, visible only in the personal difficulties, the recurring cycle of abuse, or in the mental illness of adults.

CHAPTER FIVE

Individual Work
with Sexually Abused Children

This chapter discusses the importance of a comprehensive assessment for all children who may be referred for therapy. It then suggests a practical approach which uses the regenerative model, both in assessment and in therapy, and gives some case studies to illustrate the use of the method in individual work with children.

The importance of assessment before therapy

All childcare social workers are aware of the necessity for a full assessment of a child who may be in need. The expression 'in need' refers to a child who may be in need of safeguards to promote his or her welfare. A framework for carrying out such an assessment was developed in the UK, under the guidance of the Department of Health, by the NSPCC and the University of Sheffield (Horwath 2000). As part of that framework I suggested that good communication with the child was vital and gave examples of creative and safe approaches.

Therapists who work with children will also be aware of the importance of good assessment. Assessment is usually done individually, as children are referred, although the proposed mode of therapy may be in a group. Most therapists with children recognize the importance of assessing the child's home situation before therapy is attempted. Children who have been sexually abused by a parent or carer will usually be living with a single non-abusing parent or with foster parents, adoptive parents or with professional carers and other abused children. Clearly some individual assessments of the parental figure(s), their relationship with the child, and their ability to give support, will be important. Effective and thorough assessment of children and their carers before therapy is also vital because of children's vulnerability, as was suggested in the last chapter. Although therapy with an adult will always be more successful if the individual is living in a supportive environment, therapy with a child should not be attempted unless there is some guarantee of support for the therapy within the home.

One example of the importance of this was in my own work with Karen, many years ago. (This was briefly mentioned by me at the end of the previous chapter.) She had been referred for therapy by her social worker when she was 12 years old. The information which I was given by the social worker was that she had been living with her present foster carers, together with her two younger sisters, for about two years. I was told that her birth mother was a drug user and when Karen had been living at home her mother was unable to provide the necessary care and attention. Karen often had to care for her young siblings in her mother's absence. All the children had suffered physical abuse and neglect and in addition Karen had been sexually abused by a friend of her mother's. Karen and her siblings were taken into care eventually, when she was about seven or eight.

The foster parents had coped well with the children until Karen reached puberty and began to 'act out' with aggressive behaviour. Karen was referred to me by the social worker, as a matter of urgency, because the foster parents were stating that they could not cope with her. They had asked for her to be removed and they were not keen to attend for assessment, partly because they saw Karen's behaviour as something which was a result of her difficult past and which could be 'cured' with treatment. In addition, they were, of course, extremely occupied with work and the care of the other siblings and had little time to spare.

My assessment of Karen herself went well but my assessment of her carers was rushed and inadequate. They declared their support of the therapy although it was clear that Karen's attachment to her foster mother was probably ambivalent. Her relationship with her foster father was a distant one although not hostile. He had a job which demanded long hours. It was clear that the foster mother needed more support and the over-busy social worker was unable to provide this. Both foster parents were fearful that Karen's noisy outbursts would upset the younger children who might also become 'difficult to handle'.

In retrospect it is clear that this was not the right time for therapy. The social worker had realized the problem within the home and was actively trying to find a new placement for Karen, with the agreement of the foster parents, and Karen herself. However, this was likely to take time so I agreed to see Karen for another six sessions, after the initial six assessment sessions, with the possibility that she could then have more individual sessions or be referred to a group run by my colleagues. I arranged to see the foster mother, with the social worker, for ongoing, regular discussions of Karen's progress.

Karen spent most of the first six sessions with me constructing walls and fences. Sometimes these were enclosures built from cushions, into which she placed soft toys and other objects. Sometimes they were miniature enclosures, made with toy fences and enclosing small wild animals. Occasionally she would talk about her birth mother and blame herself for 'letting them take me into care'. She felt she should have been able to care for her two sisters and for her mother too, even though she was only about seven years old at the time. As she talked she sometimes became angry and thumped cushions, although she never identified the cushions in any way. Sometimes she looked very sad and at these times she would say that she wanted to look after her mother. I felt that she was having difficulty identifying her emotions and was quite unable to express feelings satisfactorily. I assumed that the fences enclosing the wild animals were boundaries which protected her deepest feelings of anger. It was no surprise when she told me that she was not allowed to mention her previous experiences in her new home and her relationship with her foster parents seemed to be one where, once again, Karen acted as the parentified child, protecting the parents from painful feelings.

It is likely that Karen's attachment to her birth mother was dysfunctional, and disorganized (Howe 2000). As a hard drug user her mother may not often have been physically present, and when she was, she may have been a frightening or frightened figure in whom Karen could not trust, nor depend on. Attachment is, of course, concerned with the regulation of affect and this is accomplished by the mother's constant responses to the child, modulating emotions and experiences to help the child to assimilate them. There was no other constant figure to whom Karen could have attached, although there were a number of different partners of her mother who seem to have provided some caretaking, but at least one also abused her. When

Karen told her mother about the sexual abuse she was not believed, or supported.

Karen's representation of herself, her identity, and especially her emotions, had not therefore become fully formed during her first seven years of life. She may well have formed attachments to her young sisters and it was good that they were fostered together, but unfortunately I learned from Karen that the foster parents constantly denigrated her and compared her unfavourably with her sisters. Karen's view of herself was that she was unworthy, that she had unacceptable feelings such as anger, and that she was helpless to change anything. This view of her identity is typical of a child with disorganized attachment behaviour.

Although Karen found it difficult to be expressive in the sessions I can remember more than one session where she said that she was going to 'kill the dragon'. She chose a small dinosaur and enacted a scene where she enclosed herself, represented by a small girl figure, within fences and the dragon prowled around outside. At intervals she would jump up and over the fence, beating the dinosaur so that he fell down. Eventually she declared that he was dead. The futility of interpreting the metaphors in children's therapy may be illustrated by the following. At the time I remembered thinking that perhaps 'the dragon' represented the drugs which had her mother in their power. Karen had talked mainly about her mother in therapy and had not talked about the men friends (including her abuser). I did not, of course, share any interpretation with her.

Some eight years later I was able to meet up with Karen and to ask her about her memories of the therapy with myself and my colleagues. She remembered the sessions very well and I asked her if she remembered what 'the dragon' represented. Without hesitation she declared that he represented the man who had sexually abused her. She told me that she remembered 'beating him up in the sessions' and that this gave her relief and satisfaction. She said: 'It was good that I could do that because otherwise I was just being angry with other people who didn't deserve it.'

I ventured to suggest, in the more recent interview, that one of Karen's current problems at the time of her therapy was having to contain emotions which were not acceptable to her foster parents. 'Spot on,' she replied. 'I didn't realize at the time, I thought it was just me that was not acceptable.' I reminded her that at the time I had asked the social worker to try to find therapeutic support for her foster mother, which I felt should be quite separate from the work Karen was doing with myself. I had been conscious that Karen was finding it difficult to trust me and was anxious to know that I would not tell her foster parents what was happening in the sessions.

In my reports from that time I made it clear that Karen did her most productive work through painting, and this is compatible with the fact that her abuse seems to have begun very early in her life, when her memories would have been iconic and her play was 'embodiment and projected'. Through creative art work she began to express her pain and sorrow and also her anger with her mother and the man who abused her. She also demonstrated her difficulties with identity as she began to talk about how frightening this man had been. In her pictures she showed a terrifying figure with a smaller figure attached and she said this was her abuser and herself. She said that she was not only frightened, but was frightening to others. This shows how she had been confused by the person who provided some protection but who also abused her. She had dealt with it by projective identification, splitting off some of the frightening parts of this man and accepting them herself.

One of Karen's greatest worries when she saw me at the age of 12 was that she was mad, or insane. Again this could have been her way of coping with her mother's 'insane' behaviour when she had been using drugs. Karen had internalized this and it had helped to form her perceptions of herself as helpless. She was also very worried about physical damage caused to her by the men who abused her. Again this was part of the stigma and defilement she felt, and this was not totally relieved by a sensitive medical examination in which she was reassured. Karen's behaviour was often rejecting, reflecting her expectations in close relationships.

After our 12 individual sessions Karen told me that she 'could not cope with this any more'. Even though we were working through metaphor she may have felt the sessions were too intense, particularly as she was having to contain the work and was not able to share it with her foster parents. I agreed with her and asked if she would in the future be interested in joining a group for sexually abused girls, which was being run by some colleagues. She was keen to join this group which was run on creative therapy principles, mostly using dramatherapy. Before the group began, Karen was moved to a more satisfactory placement where she was able to express her difficulties.

The dramatherapist for the group remembers that although Karen appeared 'streetwise' she had the impression that, underneath, she was a little girl. 'She used to barricade herself behind cushions when we sat together in a circle; I think she felt threatened by the intensity of the experience.' The dramatherapist goes on: 'That isn't to say that she didn't engage, paradoxically. During the actual work [with stories] Karen was right in there.' It would seem, therefore, that Karen still felt the need to express her isolation and necessity for keeping herself safe in the group, as she had done in the individual sessions. However, the dramatherapy overcame those boundaries, as had the art work in my sessions.

Karen remembered, at our later interview, that she had been afraid of 'opening up' during the sessions with me, because she thought that her foster parents would learn what she had said. She remembered that we had discussed confidentiality but that she had learned to trust no one. Similarly, in the group, she had been afraid to show her feelings. 'The situation was not really safe, at home', she said, 'so it wouldn't matter what anyone did. I would fight you. It's a shame!' She acknowledged, however, that during the creative work she just enjoyed herself and she continued to attend sessions because, as she said, 'I felt relaxed, I don't know why.'

Karen's predicament illustrates the extensive damage caused to young children by abuse and neglect, and the difficulty of repairing that damage in therapy. The difficulties of finding suitable foster placements for such children are also illustrated. Karen's comments also illustrate the fact that therapy can only be successful when a child is feeling safe enough to receive it. During the individual sessions Karen was not feeling safe in her foster placement and so she could not tolerate more than 12 sessions. In the group she was just settling in with her new foster mother. The group was limited to 12 sessions and Karen seems to have coped well with this structure, attending each session regularly. It may be that she gained more from the group but whether this was due to the structure or from the fact that she was in a different placement is difficult to say.

In retrospect Karen feels that the benefits of therapy were limited to the fun she had expressing herself creatively. I can remember that at the time one of the reasons she wanted to join the group was so that she could meet other girls who had experienced sexual abuse. It may be that her stigma was reduced, therefore, during and after the group. Perhaps most of all, this retrospective study illustrates the theory that therapy cannot be imposed. It has many dimensions and trust in the therapist is vital, but with a child this may be impossible to gain if the child is not also supported outside the therapy.

My purpose in including this case study here is to show that an inadequate assessment may result in expending resources which could have been better spent on a child who was in a more suitable placement. I believe that my willingness to work with this young girl was more about my own wish to offer her something to 'make up' for the lack of attention she was being given, and less about her need to receive therapy at that time. I do not believe that the therapy did any damage and she herself thought it was useful but it is apparent, on discussing the matter with her later, that she was unable to benefit very much from it at the time.

I subsequently devised a more thorough assessment procedure, using the regenerative model, as detailed below. The regenerative model (see Figure 1.1) is in three phases: assessment, action and resolution. It is Phase One, Assessment, which will be discussed here. The model uses creative action and therapeutic methods throughout each phase.

Phase One – Assessment

Development

The purpose of assessing a child's development is to assist the therapist in understanding how this has been damaged by the trauma that the child has suffered. It may also give some indication of when abuse or neglect first occurred, bearing in mind that some children have been multiply abused by different carers. As I explained in Chapter One, Moreno's theory of child development is in three stages:

1.   Finding identity or feelings.

2.   Recognizing the self.

3.   Recognizing the other.

During the first stage the child is asking the question 'What do I feel?' and the main carer, through the attachment process, is regulating and confirming those feelings. Moreno calls this 'doubling', whereby the attachment figure expresses and regulates feelings for the child. Babies understand these feelings through their bodies and so 'embodiment play' (Jennings 1993, 1995) dominates the child's behaviour. Babies explore their own bodies and bodily secretions, experiencing sensations of touch, and also move their bodies, experiencing the associated sensations with movement. Later on, embodiment play may be expressed in the use of paints, clay, and water, or in sports or dancing.

In the second stage the child asks the question 'Who am I?' and begins to recognize and build personal identity. Caregivers reflect back the child's behaviour through 'mirroring' and children thus begin to understand how their own behaviour affects that of others. Although embodiment play continues, 'projected play' begins at this time and children become interested in dolls and other toys. Children have difficulty in holding conflicting feelings. Melanie Klein (1975) developed the concept of 'splitting', in which the baby protects 'good feelings' from 'bad feelings'. An infant may not be able to conceptualize the fact that such feelings may emanate from the same source (the carer) and is unable to handle the idea that the parent who provides food, warmth and nurture (and on whom the child is totally dependent) may also be the parent who physically abuses, or leaves the child hungry and cold. The child splits these feelings both in itself and in the significant other. This splitting leads to the psychological defence or coping mechanism of projection. The 'feel bad' part of the infant's ego may be projected onto available external objects such as toys. A teddy bear, for instance, can become 'the bad person' who is responsible for misdemeanours and who holds the angry or sad feelings which are uncomfortable for the child to acknowledge.

This theory links with Winnicott's idea of a transitional object (Winnicott 1971, 1974) which is treasured by the infant. If contacts with the infant are very inconsistent or mainly abusive and traumatic it may be that this process of 'splitting' is distorted and a vulnerable child may conceive of herself as 'all bad' in order to protect the nurturing part of her primary carer, who then becomes 'all good'. This may be a necessary survival mechanism. It is illustrated by Karen, mentioned earlier, who had assumed that as a child she was 'unacceptable', i.e. 'all bad' to her foster parents who were not accepting her angry feelings. She had to believe that they were 'all good'.

The third stage of development is represented by the question 'Who are you?', in which the child begins to understand the separateness of others and their different characteristics. This is the time for role play in which the child tries out roles such as 'mummy' or 'daddy' or perhaps a person from a fairy story or a cult figure from television. The child may integrate some of these roles within their own personality. Until this stage is reached children are unable to share because they cannot empathize with another. Most children have reached this stage by the time they start school.

By playing with a child in a child centred way (always allowing the child to take the initiative), it is usually clear which type of play dominates the child's behaviour. By the age of five most children are able to use all modes of play, but if embodiment play continues to dominate and there is little interest in other kinds of play, this is usually a sign that they have been damaged by some kind of trauma during their earliest stage of development. If projected play is included, but they are unable to take the roles of others, it may be that their abusive experiences occurred during their second stage of development.

An assessment which includes an understanding of these stages of development may assist the therapist in recognizing the extent of the damage and the length of the therapy which may be required. If a child is being assessed for a group it may be helpful to consider whether a child who is still engaged solely in embodiment play is likely to connect with children who are competent at role play. It will be seen also that a therapy which works creatively, between the therapist as attachment figure and the child, is more likely to help the child to restart their developmental process and successfully work through the three stages.

Attachment

Alongside the assessment of a child's development sits the child's capability for attaching to a caregiver and, subsequently, to the therapist. A useful list of criteria for assessing the attachment of children to their carers is given by Fahlberg (1994). This may be used alongside a wider understanding of the attachment process such as that demonstrated by Howe (1995). Howe (2000, p.156) reminds us of the four patterns of attachment which have been discovered:

1.   Secure patterns: children experience their caregiver as available and themselves positively.

2.   Ambivalent patterns: children experience their caregiver as inconsistently responsive and themselves as dependent and poorly valued.

3.   Avoidant patterns: children experience their caregivers as consistently rejecting and themselves as insecure but compulsively self-reliant.

4.   Disorganized patterns (often associated with children who have suffered severe maltreatment): children experience their caregivers as either frightening or frightened and themselves as helpless, angry and unworthy.

It should be remembered that many of the children who are being assessed for therapy because of abuse will show an insecure attachment. However, this may function quite satisfactorily for the child in the circumstances. A very few children may show no signs of attachment behaviour and clearly this would have to be nurtured with a caregiver before therapy could commence. A child with an attachment pattern which is insecure is likely to repeat the same behaviours with their therapist or their new caregiver, and to expect similar behaviour in return. However, consistent, accepting and non-threatening behaviour from a foster parent or other carer can eventually change the child's response. Often, abused children are cared for by a non-abusive parent. It may be that the person who abused the child also abused this non-abusive parent. She (for it is most often a woman) in turn may have suffered abuse or neglect in her own childhood and may have established an ambivalent or avoidant pattern of attachment to her parent, which is repeated in her child.

If therapy with the child is commenced in these circumstances it is important that support and therapy is also offered to the caregiver. In individual therapy with the child it is possible for the therapist to model consistent and accepting behaviours and for the child to adapt successfully to this.

Another, more creative way of looking at the child's attachments to significant others is to use a sociogram. Moreno (1993, pp.68–72) suggested a chart to show social configurations of a person, in time and space. I have adapted his idea for my work with children and have devised a very simple sociometric exercise to create a snapshot of a child's social configuration. It can be done with the use of small figures (animals, people, monsters, trees, fences etc.). The assessor/therapist asks the child to choose a small figure to represent themselves. Then they are asked to think about all the other people whom they know: people who lived with them or those whom they would like to live with them; 'best friends' and friends at school or in the neighbourhood; other people who are important to them (these could be teachers, relatives); not forgetting pets and, especially, people who may have died or moved away but who were still important.

The child then chooses figures to represent all these people and to make a 'snapshot' of them all, including themselves. Nowadays I usually take a photograph of this for the record, but do not give it to the child. At the end of the therapy the child is asked to repeat the process, changing things if they wish, and another photograph is taken. Comparison of the two photographs may give an indication of change, before or after therapy. The initial exercise may be a starting point for individual therapy. 'Melanie', for instance, put herself right at the outer edge of a configuration which included her parents at the centre and other extended family members around. Her 'nearest' contact was a relative who actually lived 3000 miles away. Within the immediate family grouping, instead of herself, she had put 'cuddly animals' to represent a baby and a cat whom, she said, she had 'made up'. It seemed that the baby and/or the cat were representations of herself and she was demonstrating where she wished to be, rather than where she actually felt she was (see examples of 'before and after' sociograms of children, in Chapter Eight).

Coping strategies

When children are being abused they develop coping strategies as part of their adaptive behaviour. As I have mentioned earlier these are often extreme and sometimes related to gender. More boys than girls adapt by using very controlling behaviour to cope with their feelings of powerlessness. More girls than boys use victim behaviour for the same reason. Gender socialization encourages more aggressive behaviour from males but both strategies serve the same purpose. Of course, most children will try out very controlling or very submissive, clingy behaviour from time to time but children who have been traumatized are likely to settle at the more extreme ends of this behavioural spectrum. Occasionally too the bully, in particular, changes roles and becomes the helpless victim.

These behaviours may be assessed through play when the urge to dominate or be the victim of others will easily become apparent. Naturally, during creative play, the behaviour of the child towards the therapist is also likely to be extreme. Caregivers are also likely to report coping behaviours, especially if they are controlling. Another way of assessing coping behaviours is through a simple test with the child. The B/G-Steem test (Maines and Robinson 1988) not only assesses the child's self-esteem but also the locus of control. A child with a very high score on the internal locus of control will be more controlling, whereas a child who feels a permanent victim will score high on the external locus of control. Naturally, children who are at the extreme ends of this spectrum will be unsuitable for group therapy and should be seen on an individual basis.

Safety

The final part of the assessment process, using the regenerative model, is the assessment of safety for the child. As I have stated, no therapy is possible if a child is still under threat of some kind from an abuser or abusers. As I have also shown by the case study of Karen, therapy is less than effective if the work is not well supported by the child's caregivers. Therapy could also be unsafe if the caregivers cannot understand how vulnerable the child is during therapy sessions, and for some time afterwards.

The child's ability to self-protect is also important, to help prevent further abuse, but, as I have said, this should not be taught in a stereotypical way because there is a danger that children will feel that they are to blame because they did not prevent the abuse. If the child is felt to be in danger of further abuse (from outside the caregiving family) then safety should be discussed with the carers, together with the child. As the therapy draws to a close it may be that some children will still need special attention to their personal safety.

This thorough assessment, which may take several weeks, lays the foundations for Phase Two of the model, the Action. It should be possible to ascertain by this time whether the child is most suitable for individual one-to-one therapy, or whether the child is ready for a group. For a group the therapist has to assess whether the child's development is such that she is able to cope with other children who have been abused. If relationship skills are inappropriate to chronological age then some individual work may be needed first. In addition, of course, if a child's coping skills include heavy controlling and abusive behaviour then he or she will also need individual work before a group can be attempted. Assessment for groupwork is also discussed in the next chapter.

Working with individual children

Many of the traumatized children whom we see for therapy have been living for years in home situations where they have had little or no individual attention. When this is given by the therapist the child undoubtedly benefits. As I have stated, therapy is enhanced if the child also has a healthy attachment to a caregiver. Indeed, research has shown (Cawson 2002) that such attachments and support networks can even reduce the impact on the child from abuse. A similar, functional, attachment can be made between the therapist and child and this forms the basis for the therapy which recreates the developmental processes which have been delayed or distorted in the child. This creative interaction occurs in 'the space between' the two protagonists, therapist and child, just as it occurs for most children between the original attachment figure and the child. As I explained in Chapter Two, 'the space between' is necessary to encourage the links between body and mind, and between the left and right hemispheres of the brain. Using play, metaphor and symbolism will facilitate the method. To show how the model can be adapted for children of different ages, I will give examples of work with a six-year-old boy and an 11-year-old girl.

Joe

This six-year-old had been abused by his maternal uncle while he lived in the house together with Joe and Sharon, his mother. After Joe had disclosed the abuse, initially to a teacher, Sharon also disclosed that she had been abused by the same elder brother for many years. Despite this (or perhaps because of it), Sharon had found it difficult to object when her brother moved into the house after Joe's father had left, some two or three years previously. Sharon had received some practical support from her own mother but this was withdrawn when Joe made his accusations. Her brother promptly moved back to live with his mother. Although Joe's abuser had been brought to trial there was insufficient evidence to convict him and so Joe and Sharon were ostracized by the rest of the family. While Joe came for his therapy, his mother also received therapy in her own right. In addition she received community support. She said that Joe's teacher (to whom he had disclosed the abuse) had said that Joe often appeared to be 'daydreaming' during class, and that he sometimes became uncontrollably angry with other children.

At assessment Joe enjoyed messy play and sometimes played creatively with the glove puppets. Occasionally he would dress up into a Superman character who was very controlling, but he was unable to hold this role for more than a few minutes. As therapy progressed he played in the sand tray and repeatedly buried cars and people. He seemed to be creating a scene of devastation and he did not seem to show any emotion as he remarked that 'all the people are dead so we don't know what happened'. The therapist stayed with the sandplay for some weeks, occasionally 'doubling' for one of the buried figures and expressing sadness or distress as Joe piled on more sand so that the figure was completely covered. The therapist shared with her supervisor that it was difficult not to try to move the action forward but at the same time she recognized that Joe did not appear to be ready for this. The supervisor agreed and suggested that she stayed with the embodiment play and do as much doubling as possible for all the buried figures and for Joe.

The therapist's patience was rewarded as she continued to double for Joe, helping him to begin to express emotions for the first time. After a while he spontaneously chose one of the glove puppets as 'a friend'. 'Spot', a dog puppet, seemed to be a witness, a silent supporter, as Joe quietly but determinedly continued to bury figures in the sand. His mother had said that she was worried because Joe sometimes became 'unreasonably angry' and destroyed toys and even attacked her or his friends. Joe seemed very worried about expressing anger in the sessions but eventually he began to focus on another of the puppets in the playroom. His concentration upon embodiment play was now moving towards projected play.

The glove puppet was a hippopotamus and Joe said it was 'horrible'. They played with this and with other puppets for some time. The therapist then asked him if he had anything to say to 'Horrible Hippo'. 'Won't speak to him,' Joe replied. The therapist placed 'Horrible Hippo' on top of a large bean bag. 'What has he done?' she asked. Joe thumped his fist on top of the bean bag. 'Horrible, horrible stuff to kids.' 'He's not allowed to do that,' said the therapist. 'It makes me angry.' Carefully, without losing control, she began to mirror angry behaviour for Joe, picking up a 'hitting stick' (rolled-up newspaper secured with tape) and hitting the bean bag with one hearty 'Thwack!'.

Almost immediately Joe took the stick from the therapist and began to hit the bean bag, including the puppet. Her patient 'doubling' behaviour, followed by 'mirroring' of Joe's anger, helped him to move into expression of feelings. The therapist watched Joe carefully to check that he could handle his anger. A premature expression of anger by the therapist could have been anti-therapeutic and could have caused Joe to go back into alternately repressing his anger and inappropriately expressing it against friends. Joe continued to hit the bean bag until he became tired and the therapist suggested that he might like to sit down.

Joe picked up his supportive 'Spot' and sat comfortably in a corner. 'Me and him did for him,' he remarked, looking with satisfaction at the collapsed Hippo. The therapist reminded Joe that it was all right to be angry but that it was not 'OK' to hit real people. 'I know,' said Joe. After this session Joe seemed much more able to hold his 'Superman' role. He spent many sessions in this role, rescuing children from monsters and dragons. In the feedback sessions with his mother, Sharon, she said that his angry behaviour had subsided but he had asked her how they could get 'Grandma' to understand what had happened. The therapist offered to organize a joint meeting with the grandmother, Sharon and Joe but, unfortunately, the grandmother refused to attend.

Despite this, Joe's behaviour continued to improve and Sharon was pleased with the outcome. She acknowledged that her own therapy had helped her to understand how she was unavailable for Joe when he was a baby. Her own memories of abuse and domestic violence had made it difficult for her to form an attachment with him. She was now enjoying their relationship and beginning to forge a new life for them both, separately from her family.

Holly

Eleven-year-old Holly was suffering from 'bad dreams'. Her history was that she had been sexually abused by her mother's boyfriend over a period of years, from when she was about two years old. She was now living with her mother, Mary, and their relationship was improving greatly. Holly and Mary were of Afro-Caribbean descent but were living in an area which was mostly white.

During assessment it was suggested that Holly might like to keep a journal so that she could make notes about the 'bad dreams' if she wished, and then work on them during the therapy sessions. It was realized by the therapist that most of the 'bad dreams' occurred during the day and were, in fact, dissociated episodes, or 'flashbacks', of the abuse she had suffered.

Holly and the therapist made an agreement to work on any dreams that came up, for six sessions, and that this could be extended if Holly wanted that. This time boundary seemed to be important for Holly who, although she wanted to work on the dreams, felt very apprehensive about doing so. She said that she 'tried to push them [the dreams] down, but they keep popping up'. The therapist talked to Holly about having some control of the dreams, and suggested she brought them up deliberately in the sessions, then she would be in control. She could change the dreams if she wished, during the sessions. Holly would almost certainly have been dissociating during the abuse because of its horrific content and the fact that she was extremely young when it occurred. However, she continued to use the word 'dreams' rather than 'flashbacks' to describe the occurrences, and said they mostly happened at night when she was in bed. The therapist therefore continued to use the word 'dreams' when working with Holly.

Because of Holly's worries about time boundaries, it was also agreed that the 'dreamwork' would take a maximum of 20 minutes each session, preceded and followed by about ten minutes of preparation and closing down. It is important that the child's attention span is taken into consideration and her fears about addressing the material itself are addressed. Any kind of therapy must always be with the consent of the child and for this type of psychodramatic work the child must feel ready to address the specific content. Holly had formed an attachment with the therapist over a long period of assessment and had specially asked to do this work.

The therapist explained, during the warm-up, that Holly could stop the drama at any time and that sometimes she and the therapist would play various parts, and sometimes she could use the large soft toys, puppets or small figures which were in the room. Holly immediately picked out a miniature dinosaur and said, 'That can be him.' She chose a very small child figure for herself. She said that the dream was 'what happened lots of times since I was two'. The scene which she then showed, with the miniature figures, was horrific. The small figure which represented herself had been immobilized in a particularly cruel way. It was a moment frozen in time, like a photograph. It seemed to be direct from her iconic memory. It was obvious that the only way in which it could be re-enacted was to miniaturize it, as she had done instinctively.

Holly put her trainer-clad foot on the plastic dinosaur saying, 'I'm squashing it.' She asked the therapist to put it in the waste bin since she did not want to touch it. She was obviously deeply affected by the scene and did not want to look at it further. After a short period of reassuring talk she moved into action again which projected into the future. The therapist asked Holly to move along an imaginary line where she became older, and which took her through her teenage years. She reversed roles with the therapist so that she could look at herself whilst she was growing up. She talked about her fears and her strengths and gave 'herself' (therapist in role) good advice about protecting herself. She felt she could now see 'men like him' more clearly than most people and that she was, therefore, stronger and wiser than her mother had been (although she emphasized her mother's support now). She wanted to protect other children also.

Each subsequent session, like the first one, described one picture which seemed frozen in time, in which Holly herself was completely helpless. She was clear that she was describing things that had happened, but that 'kept coming back as dreams'. They seldom appeared to contain metaphor but were true iconic flashbacks into her unconscious. Each flashback was accompanied by a heightened affect during which her face appeared very vulnerable, and as she spoke, her voice was shaky.

In another session Holly again described a picture in which she was immobilized, this time using a small, stuffed, pink pig to represent herself, and the dinosaur for the abuser. She said, 'She wants to tell her mum but she is too frightened.' She was asked, as she had been before, if she wanted to change the picture and this time she said she did. She said she would be a police inspector and the therapist could be the sergeant. She handed imaginary handcuffs to the police sergeant, while she picked up a cosh (rolled-up newspaper). She and the sergeant flexed their muscles to show how strong they were.

The scene Holly had set up, with the pig and the dinosaur, remained in the room and she enacted bursting through an imaginary door, 'coshing' the dinosaur and instructing the sergeant to 'put the 'cuffs on him'. She covered the pink pig carefully with a blanket, picking her up and saying she was taking her to a safe place. She then 'fed' the pig with drink and biscuits, cradling her softly and reassuring her. She looked over to the dinosaur, who still lay handcuffed and unconscious in the room. She instructed her sergeant, 'Wake him up! Take him to prison, and tie him down in a cell.' The sergeant obeyed. Holly shouted verbal abuse at the dinosaur, whilst still cradling the pink pig in the safe place, telling him of all the damage he had done to her, to her mother and to other children. The words spilled from her, it was a catharsis. She asked the sergeant also to tell the man what damage he had done. The therapist, whilst doing this, was struck by the reversal of roles as the dinosaur, Holly's abuser, was thus humiliated and completely helpless and immobilized in the way she had been. Still in role as the inspector, Holly threw the dinosaur out of the room.

After this session Holly set up scenes which she explained 'were not real dreams, because I'm not asleep, they're kind of dreams when you're awake'. She thus acknowledged the truth about the flashbacks which she may have felt too embarrassed to discuss before. She enacted a flashback where her abuser appeared in her bedroom sitting on the furniture. She was very clear that her mother, at the present time, was able to be extremely supportive and strong and was very protective. However, her mother had not been able to be supportive at the time of the abuse. Holly now wanted her mother to come into the room where her abuser was sitting on the furniture and to rescue her. She role-reversed into her mother and rescued herself (played by a soft hedgehog this time). She then said she was 'Wonder-Mum!' and the therapist became Holly, and together they dispatched the dinosaur from the room (actually behind the drawn blinds in the room). 'Splat!' she said as they mimed throwing him out of the window, wiping her hands free of all traces. Holly then said that a policeman was waiting outside and she reversed herself into the police role. As is usual with children, she directed most of the scene herself and reversed into other roles without direction from the therapist. She announced that she was taking the offender to hospital and then he would be going to jail for the rest of his life.

The therapist then asked Holly to reverse back into herself so that the therapist could play the police role. She did this, but before either of them spoke she looked up at the 'policeman' and said, 'Sorry.' The therapist asked her what she was sorry for. 'I don't know, it just came out when I went back to being me.' The therapist, now back in role as herself, said 'I'm wondering why you feel you need to say sorry', and Holly answered, 'Because it was my fault, I let him do those things.' The therapist said that the scene with the police was closed, and she used the mirror technique to allow Holly to look at the relative size and power of herself and her abuser. Holly chose to build a tower of chairs and cushions for him and a soft toy for herself. She and the therapist worked together in role play about children obeying adults and she told the therapist about the threats the abuser had made. Nevertheless, her feelings of guilt were still around.

During the next few weeks they continued to work on Holly's feelings. She said the 'dreams' were getting much less frequent but were still occurring. On one occasion she found it helpful when the therapist reversed into her role during an abuse situation which she had set up with stuffed toys. The therapist kept still and kept her mouth closed, making very small noises of distress. As she came out of role she shared with Holly that she had felt frozen and unable to speak. Holly looked surprised and said that was exactly how she had felt. She began to understand a little more about her feelings of guilt. They rehearsed empowerment scenes where she was not 'frozen' and could shout and tell someone.

The therapist was concerned about the 'contamination' of Holly's new safe bedroom, where most, but not all, of the flashbacks had occurred. They set up a scene to represent her bedroom and Holly suggested that a small army of teddies could be 'on guard' to 'make it safe'. They set up one small teddy and several imaginary ones in strategic points about the scene until she felt it was quite safe. Afterwards she was allowed to take the small teddy home. Towards the end of the six agreed sessions, Holly felt she needed two more because she was still feeling 'a bit guilty about the abuse'.

The therapist asked Holly to become 'a good mum' and to talk to herself, aged three. She chose a small hedgehog for herself, which the therapist doubled, during the enactment. The therapist (in role as Holly) said that she thought that the abuse was her own fault because she had not called out while it was happening. As 'good mum', Holly said, 'You could not, because you were frozen.' The therapist then said she should have told someone afterwards. As mum, Holly replied, 'But you didn't understand that then, you were too little.' They then reversed roles so that Holly could experience this as herself.

In the last session Holly said that she had only had one 'dream' during that week but that she had 'done it herself'. She was asked to explain. She said that after the flashback she had re-enacted it using soft toys, and changing the outcome. She said that she had felt better afterwards because 'the dream only did what I wanted it to do'. The therapist asked her which toy she had chosen for her abuser and she said it was a teddy she did not like and which lived at the bottom of a cupboard. This was Holly's very individual way of coping but it felt as if she was at least controlling the flashbacks and not being dominated by them. It seemed that she had made another step in her journey towards self healing.

Conclusion

Both Holly and Joe were suffering from complex post-traumatic stress disorder (Herman 1992) when they were referred to their therapists. Neither of them were able to regulate their emotions and both had suffered trauma during their early years, when their attachments were tenuous or dysfunctional. Both were still suffering from dissociative episodes. Both had difficulties in their self-perception and Holly certainly was full of shame, guilt and stigma. Neither of them had good relationships with others and their sense of self-protection was impaired.

All the above symptoms are part of the diagnosis of complex PTSD and they are also signs that early development was damaged. For instance, both Joe and Holly sometimes found it difficult to express their feelings or they expressed these inappropriately. Both had problems with their own identity and with their relationships with others. Each therefore found it difficult to answer the questions 'What do I feel?', 'Who am I?' and 'Who are you?' as suggested earlier in this chapter.

During the therapy they each made good relationships, similar to attachments, with the therapist, who in each case worked creatively at a level with which they could cope. The 'space between' was respected in the use of metaphor, the use of toys and the atmosphere of play. Each child and his/her therapist created situations jointly which helped to express feelings, confirm identity and forge relationships. Both therapists used 'doubling', 'mirroring' and 'role reversal' as part of their repertoire. Both Joe and Holly are representative of many children with similar difficulties who have been helped through creative therapy intervention. They may need further therapy or support as they reach another stage in their development, at adolescence perhaps, but it seems that after creative therapy they are better equipped to face whatever the future brings.

CHAPTER SIX

Groupwork with Sexually Abused Children

This chapter describes in detail two groups for sexually abused children (aged between 8 and 11) which were set up, with the co-operation of the NSPCC, for the purposes of research. Some aspects of the first group (the pilot group) have been partly described in a chapter in *Psychodrama with Trauma Survivors* (Bannister in Kellermann and Hudgins 2000). Both the pilot group and the main group will be described here with emphasis on the practicality of working in this mode with staff who are accustomed to working with traumatized children, but who have received a minimum of specialist training. All therapeutic groups with children should have at least two therapists because of responsibility for safety which each therapist must carry. Childcare social workers, arts therapists, child psychologists and psychotherapists, and other professionals may form a team in which their skills and expertise are shared.

In the research project a total of eight staff (from the above professional groups) received a few hours of extra training on the regenerative model, and spent some time together building rapport and practising their creative skills. In particular, they practised techniques of 'doubling', 'mirroring' and 'role reversal'. It was helpful that representatives from statutory and voluntary bodies, including health professionals, were working together. Two therapists were used in each group, although for the purposes of research an extra person sat as an observer through the sessions, taking verbatim notes. It had been decided not to use video cameras to document the sessions because of the risk that some children may have been the victims of abusers who had used cameras. In the event this was seen to be a wise decision. Staff worked on a rota basis in the groups so that all of them gained experience in the method, but only two therapists (usually a male and a female) ran each group of boys and girls.

Phase One – Assessment

As explained in Chapter Four, the assessment of each child before therapy is important and, following the regenerative model, this was done by looking at the four areas of development, attachment, coping strategies and safety. For both groups the staff team liaised with statutory social work teams in the area asking for referrals of sexually abused boys and girls of primary school age (5 to 11). For practical, developmental reasons it was decided to select children from a two-year age band, depending on the majority of suitable children who were referred.

The assessments were carried out in six steps. The first consisted of taking a full history (usually by telephone) from the referrer (the social worker), the school, any other relevant professionals, and parents. The second step consisted of a home visit by the two group therapists to see the child and parent(s) together and then the parent(s) and child separately. The third step was a repeat of this session but it took place on the premises where the group was to be held. During these visits attachment to the main caregiver could be assessed, children's developmental levels could be ascertained, and coping strategies and safety could also be determined.

In step four the two therapists compared their process notes from the interviews and shared their information from various sources. Then in the fifth step they made separate assessments regarding attachments and coping strategies before coming together again for a final decision. In the sixth step, if the child was likely to join the group, each school was approached and a teacher or headteacher was asked to complete a questionnaire on the child's behaviour (see below for full details of the assessment process).

The children

The focus of any assessment of a child for suitability for a group must always consider the effect that each child may have upon each of the others. In looking at development, for instance, we must remember that an abused child already has a sense of difference from others, so some similarity in developmental levels for all children in the group is necessary. In the pilot group each referred child was assessed separately and the therapist offered toys and equipment suitable for embodiment play, projected play or role play. As I mentioned in the previous chapter, it was important that the group should contain children who were able to use all three types of play, at least to some extent. Children who were stuck in very early play were offered individual therapy, rather than a group.

In looking at attachment the assessment team was looking for evidence of some basic attachments in the children's lives and a possibility that attachments may be formed with the therapists and also with the other children. As I have said, for the group each child was seen with a parent or caregiver, together and separately on two occasions. Assessments were made in a similar way to that described in the previous chapter, for individual work with children. A sociogram or sociometric test (Moreno 1993) was undertaken by each child, using small figurines and toys as before (see Chapter Eight for photographs).

Coping strategies were assessed using the same strategies and tests as before (Maines and Robinson 1988). As I mentioned previously, children who exhibit extreme coping strategies, whether they are over-submissive or extremely controlling, will be unsuitable for a group where they may be exploited or where they may bully other children. In a group for sexually abused children this is, of course, extremely important. Any history of abuse of other children is also important and it must be realized that sometimes this can be 'glossed over' by parents or professionals alike; discussions should be held with teachers and referring social workers as well as care-givers and children.

Safety of the child within the group is assessed partly by looking at the home situation but, more importantly for groupwork, looking at the results of the previous assessment of development, attachment and coping strate-gies. A child whose coping strategies are extremely controlling could abuse other children in the group and, conversely, a child who was very vulnerable could easily become victimized. In addition, the distance in time from the abuse, or discovery of the abuse, is important. Some children may be com-pletely unready to hear about the abuse of others in the group and may become overwhelmed. It may also be borne in mind that some children who have suffered a short period of sexual abuse outside the family may have become more vulnerable to such abuse because of temporary family difficul-ties. At such times, parents who are normally supportive may have become unavailable and the child could have been easily seduced by a powerful perpetrator. Such a child may need help in exploring the family difficulties with the family, rather than becoming a member of a group where sexual abuse is the focus.

Assessment should therefore follow the child's agenda at all times so that children are able to express feelings about anything which is worrying them. During the assessment period of several weeks, therapists need to ensure that children are reasonably secure in their family environment and that caregivers are able to support the children during the period of their therapy.

Parents / caregivers

Many children who have been sexually abused do not live with their birth parents when they come for therapy. Many are in the care of the local authority and some of these are with foster parents and others may be in small group homes. A few children may have been adopted. A large number of children, however, remain with one non-abusing parent, usually the mother. In this project the majority of the children were with their birth mothers, who were coping without a permanent partner. From a therapeutic point of view it is important that parents are supportive of the therapy and do not undermine it. It is also helpful for therapists to hear how children are behaving at home both before, during and after therapy.

Ethically, non-abusing parents have a right to be informed of the kind of treatment their child is receiving, and in this project parents and children all signed forms to say that they were aware of the nature of the groupwork and consented to the research. In the first group the mothers all stated that they were available to meet once a month with a member of the therapy team for a supportive group in which feedback could be given and received and questions answered. This provided a useful forum for an exchange of views but the group support was not as successful as we had hoped, perhaps because the women did not live in close proximity. In the main group the parents were not available to attend a support group (or did not wish to do so) and so they were visited once a month by a member of the therapy team. The parents understood the concept of group confidentiality, and if the mothers in the support group raised issues where this may cause a problem, that mother was offered individual time with the therapist.

Of course, confidentiality was part of the 'contract' which was signed by children and group leaders in the first session and this concept was carefully explained to the children. They were told that if a group leader felt that any child was still being abused, or was abusing others, then that information could not be kept confidential. Otherwise, what went on in the group was confidential, although the children were free to share with parents or others in general what kind of things were taking place in the group. In discussion children seemed clear that they understood this concept.

All the parents completed behavioural assessment forms on their children both before and after the group. The 'Strengths and difficulties questionnaire' (Goodman 1997) proved to be very suitable for this because it did not focus exclusively on 'difficult behaviour' and provided a good talking point for parents and therapists to discuss the child in a positive way. This questionnaire also has a special section for teachers that was most helpful in gaining a view of how the child behaved in school and the reports from both parents and teachers gave a rounder picture of each child.

Transport

To emphasize the importance of the groups, they were held during school time so that they would not be seen as recreational groups. The time was chosen to fit in with mothers who had to pick up other children from school afterwards. Teachers were supportive of this idea when they were approached. In the first group, the children were brought from school by their mothers or by registered volunteers who also returned them home. In the second group, one registered volunteer undertook to bring all the children and to return them later to their homes. This decision helped the group to cohere (since group interaction began from the moment the second child was picked up) and seemed to be the best solution.

Size of group

The size of the group was partly determined by the number of suitable referrals but also by the fact that young, sexually abused children need some individual attention in therapy. The methods of 'doubling' and 'mirroring' require personal action by a staff member, who will need to concentrate on one child at a time. Therefore, the number of children in each group was four and five respectively. There were at least two children of each gender in each group.

Phase Two – Action

Spontaneity and creativity

The group provided plenty of opportunities for both staff and children to be spontaneous and creative. The children devised the games with which the groups commenced and these were usually well known playground games such as 'Grandmother's footsteps'.

Puppet play was provided each week for projective, mirroring behaviour. The child used the puppet to show how they were feeling. In the younger group one girl, Sally, was seen as different from her school mates. Although outwardly she appeared similar, she had complained in the group that 'everyone knew what had happened' and that she was called sexual names by other children. She was obviously feeling the stigma of sexual abuse. She selected a puppet which was recognizably a girl but which had spiky orange hair which made her look somewhat alarming. 'I'm feeling bad 'cos I've got orange hair and no one likes me,' she said sadly, as the puppet. 'I've got no friends.' Two boys, David and Mark, immediately reacted, picking up a shark puppet and a bear, respectively. They began to fight the girl puppet. 'I'm tired of this,' said Sally, as the puppet. 'They're trying to eat me, I'm scared.' Mark, as the bear, immediately changed his tactic, saying he was 'a teddy bear who could give her a cuddle'. David hid under a cushion, with his shark. A female staff member doubled him, taking up his body posture, watching carefully but saying nothing. David responded by reacting playfully with the staff member and her puppet. Together they watched the action of the two puppets, the bear and the girl.

The girl puppet said, 'My mum and my sister and me all sleep together now in the same room because it's safe.' The bear said, 'I can keep you safe too, because I'm strong.' Sally put down her girl puppet and picked up a shark. 'I can eat people too,' she said, showing her strength by biting cushions. The two boys then picked up crocodile puppets and David said to the female staff member who had been doubling him: 'I love you.' Mark's crocodile said to Sally and the female staff member, 'I'll protect you.' David, who often showed much aggression, spoke through the crocodile. 'I won't hurt them, I'm a friend.'

It is perhaps significant that this interchange took place just over halfway through the group. The young children (eight or nine) were able to project feelings onto puppets and see their own behaviour reflected there. They were also able to reverse roles to a certain extent, the girl showing her strong, self-protective role, after she had revealed her vulnerability. The boys were able to show their loving, protective roles after they had shown their aggression.

The children in this group responded well to doubling and mirroring but at first role play and role reversal were kept strictly by them within a fairytale metaphor. When 'dressing-up' clothes were introduced, after seven sessions, the children played queens and kings or Cinderella. Mostly they wanted to play roles in which they had control. They also wanted to keep control of the story and this was easier to do when there was a named fairytale. Gradually, over the several sessions, roles became more varied and original stories were invented. Early on some of the children had made 'enclosures' from clay. They seemed to be preoccupied with boundaries (not surprisingly for children whose boundaries had been violated) and one child said that the enclosures were 'houses for pigs'. Some small plastic pigs and piglets were available in the group room and had been used in assessment exercises before the group began. This reminded the children of the story of *The Three Little Pigs*, and they asked for this story to be told during a session whilst they were playing with clay (as briefly mentioned in Chapter Three).

The traditional story was told, where the first little pig built himself a house of straw which the wolf blew down and then ate the little pig. Then the second little pig built himself a house of sticks which the wolf also managed to blow down, resulting in the second pig's demise. The third pig got wise and built himself a house of bricks. The wolf was unable to blow this down and he threatened to come down the chimney. The remaining pig built a fire and the wolf falls in it and is destroyed. This rather gruesome fairy story is often told to nursery age children who enjoy the repetitive speech, 'Little pig, little pig, let me in, let me in', and the reply, 'No, No, by the hair of my chinny-chin-chin, I will not let you in!', then the wolf's threat: 'I'll huff and I'll puff and I'll blow your house down!' Bettelheim (1976), the great psychologist who worked with fairy stories, reckoned that the story was acceptable because children recognized that each little pig represents a stage of life and so each little pig can die and move on to the next stage. I agree with his assessment, but I always go along with any change which a child suggests because this may well have meaning for him or her.

This story also carries some overtones of the experience of sexual abuse within the family. The 'wolf' abuser tries several times to attack them and at first manages to do so because their defences are not strong enough. Eventually they manage to protect themselves and to punish the abuser. However, there is no role for a protector for the piglets in this story. It is perhaps not surprising that a theme began to develop in the group about mothers who were unable (or even unwilling) to protect their children. I felt that 'mother-blaming' had probably arisen from several sources. Mothers of abused children frequently blame themselves and feel that they did not protect their children. They feel they should have known what the abuser was doing. Of course this is unrealistic and mothers are sometimes helped to cope with this guilt when the 'grooming' process, by abusers, is explained to them. They begin to see that their child has been systematically wooed by the abuser and prepared for abuse by deliberately keeping out the main protector. Sometimes mothers are also blamed by other family members or friends or even by professionals.

I decided that it might be helpful if the children could see that their mothers may also have been tricked by their abusers. I therefore used the story which the children had suggested, and the theme of 'no protection' which they had brought up, and re-wrote the story of *The Three Little Pigs* so that the wolf talks his way into the unsafe, straw home, and is trusted by the mother pig. The little pigs' suspicions are aroused when he suggests building a stronger home for them made of sticks, *with him inside it*, especially when they realize that one of the sticks is to be used for punishing them. However, their mother does not hear their warnings and they have to go along with the wolf's next suggestion that they all build a brick home. The piglets overhear Mr Wolf telling Mr Fox that he is 'on to a good thing. I've got a nice house and three little piglets, all ready to cook for my dinner.' Their mother still cannot believe their warnings and Mr Wolf duly pushes two of the little pigs into the oven while the mother is out. The third runs to get the mother who rescues them just in time. The mother pig and the three little pigs chase off the wolf together.

Just over halfway through the run of the group, this alternative story was read to the children who asked if they could 'act it out'. They spontaneously acted out several scenes, which they devised and cast, and also, at my suggestion, repeated some scenes whilst playing different roles. As is common with sexually abused children they relished playing the role of Mr Wolf, the abuser himself. Of course, this is one of the ways of coping with abuse, to take on temporarily the role of abuser instead of victim. Some were also happy to play the role of the mother and to demonstrate how easy it was to believe a very plausible Mr Wolf and to disbelieve the children. The children were also intrigued when staff members played the children, especially when they were afraid, or thwarted because mother did not believe.

At no time was this metaphor ever brought into reality, or comparisons made with real life situations. However, after the story the group was asked what they thought of the 'new' three little pigs story. Without comment Mark donned a scarf and some beads from the dressing-up box and began to dance, in the exuberant fashion of an Irish stepdancer. The others, boys and girls, quickly grabbed an item of costume (most of this consisted of pieces of material, ropes of beads and belts). They all stood close together, but not touching, and danced *Riverdance* to the accompaniment of the staff clapping or beating a drum.

It seemed that some insight had been gained by at least some of the children and the story was not forgotten. Some three sessions later during puppet play, one boy became a pig and the others immediately became pigs with one girl saying that she was the mother pig. They all moved around on hands and knees (temporarily discarding their puppets and moving into role play). One small 'piglet' picked up a wolf puppet and banged it on the ground shouting, 'I killed the big bad wolf.' The girl playing the mother pig joined in with the 'wolf-bashing', as did the other 'piglets'.

All these sessions, using dramatherapy which was spontaneously devised by the children, helped them to look at their experiences through the dramatic mirror. They were sufficiently removed from their personal experiences to feel safe, but were close enough for them to identify with the characters and to empathize with some of them. They were enabled to share experiences with each other without having to be too explicit. They illustrated some of the wider dilemmas which are faced by children who are sexually abused. It is clear that relationships with non-abusing parents were deeply damaged and that these mothers were often placed in almost impossible situations as they tried, and sometimes failed, to believe their children against the word of fathers and husbands.

Working with dreams

Sessions on dreams or flashbacks have already been described, with an individual child, during the last chapter. During these sessions the child used small figurines to represent herself and others in the dream. It is important that the child is not further traumatized by re-enactments in which she plays herself in an abusive situation. In groupwork with children it is important that a staff member (or trained psychodrama auxiliary) plays the abused child in psychodramatic re-enactments. The events are then seen 'as if in a mirror' and the child is distanced from the pain. Another safety factor is, of course, metaphor, as shown in the use of *The Three Little Pigs*.

In the main group, with older children aged from 9 to 11, the children 'warmed up' to psychodramatic action by familiar physical games and by the use of puppet play to facilitate expression of feelings. After a break there was a period of 45 minutes which was usually filled with art work or other creative play. We always allowed 15 minutes for 'group sharing' and winding down after creative activity so our psychodramatic enactments never lasted more than 30 minutes. This seems to be sufficient for children of this age although work with adolescents can run to an hour.

One girl, Liz, asked if she could work on her dreams and the group agreed. She had said that she was having trouble sleeping since she was afraid of having the dream again. She began to narrate the dream:

> I was walking, we were on holiday. I was walking back to the hotel when the ground started shaking. It was a volcano which had started erupting. Then I was swimming in the hotel pool but I got out and mum said, 'Jump in the car!' But the lava was already flowing and a lava ball came through the car roof and burnt…[her younger brother], who died. Then mum got killed and…[her older brother] was very badly injured. Dad and I got him on the plane but he died later.

The scenario of the volcanic eruption seemed to be a perfect metaphor for what had happened in Liz's family. Where one sibling abuses another there are inevitable splits within family members and there are often several 'casualties'. The reactions of the authorities are also very important and often it seems as if the abusing child becomes much more of a focus than the victim.

However, this metaphor seemed to be too powerful for the group to handle. Although the staff member was ready to take Liz's role the rest of the group appeared paralysed. The theme of death and destruction was, perhaps, their own worse nightmare. However, it was important that Liz did not feel guilty for bringing this theme to the group and so I suggested that, to miniaturize and project it, we should use puppets to act out the dream. This suggestion was received very enthusiastically by the whole group who immediately grabbed puppets and co-operated completely as Liz directed them in the re-enactment, with which Liz appeared satisfied. I then asked Liz if she could 'change the dream' and she changed it to another holiday scene with her whole family, in which they were all in the pool, the 'tremor' of the volcano only created a wave, which the whole family dealt with easily, and then they all 'went to McDonalds for a meal'. Food metaphors appear frequently in the dreams which children enact!

So the drama was distanced by metaphor, by projection and miniaturization, and in this way Liz gained some control, with the help of the group. She reported some weeks later that the dream had not re-appeared. All the children asked if they too could re-enact dreams. Ned said that his dream was about playing out with friends on a winter evening, just before dark, when a man came and took away his best friend. It seemed that Ned had automatically designated a best friend as the victim, instead of himself, and I felt that this projection was quite acceptable for him, and the group. Ned then chose a large floor cushion for 'the man'. He pulled it with his foot and placed it in position at the edge of the group of children. He took over the direction himself (as Liz had done), kicking the cushion around the group to show how 'the man' was prowling around the children. 'The man' then grabbed the best friend and took him away.

In changing the action Ned decided that he wanted the group to continue playing, ignoring the man, so that he would go away. This was replayed and the group enthusiastically concentrated on playing a game whilst ignoring 'the man'. This seemed to be a good example of receiving support from the group, both in the therapeutic situation and in his real life situation at home and school, with his friends. Ned's mother and his teacher said that during the group he began to widen his circle of friends at school and, in particular, he chose some 'strong' boys to be part of his group as well as the younger, quieter children who had previously been his friends.

Suzie was anxious to replay her dream and the following week she set the scene carefully, saying that she was grown up in the dream, and that she was in a bedroom. She told the story first before the enactment, and said that she had just had an argument with a man, a friend, who had now left her alone. Another man, dressed as a clown and carrying a knife, suddenly jumped out of the wardrobe and stabbed her. Suzie hit him with a bottle and tried to run out of the room. Another man, a cleaner, was cleaning the floor outside the room, and she asked him to help her but 'he could not hear her because he was completely deaf'. Suzie looked dejected and completely powerless at this point. I was, of course, struck by the metaphor of profound deafness which illustrates the position of 'no one wanting to hear' when a child has been abused.

The children re-enacted the dream with a staff member playing Suzie. Jane, who had developed a special friendship with Suzie, surprised the group by asking if she could play the clown. I felt that she was perhaps needing to try the abuser role instead of her usual victim role in life. Suzie stood by my side during this enactment, watching carefully, and then said confidently that she wanted to play the scene differently and she wanted to play herself. In the re-enactment she directed the cleaner, played by Ned, to 'hear' and to help her. He did so enthusiastically, disposing of the clown with his own (imaginary) knife. Again this was a case of a very victimized child, Ned, taking an opposite role. The group then joined together in a circle for sharing their thoughts and feelings about both re-enactments. Jane was carefully de-roled from playing the clown and Ned from playing the cleaner. It is important to note that neither Jane nor Ned was in the abuser role for more than a few seconds and that each of these two vignettes only took about ten minutes each, from start to finish.

In staff discussions afterwards we realized that this may have been the first time that Suzie had been truly 'heard' with regard to her abuse. She had been abused with others, including her older sister, by a neighbour. She had not given evidence because the older children had done so. Her father had found the episode very difficult to handle so it is likely that it had not been discussed openly at home. Her father had felt violent towards the abuser but had, of course, been restrained from action by his wife. Suzie was usually very controlling in the group but in the re-enactment of the dream she was able to take the opposite role and to ask for help and to receive it. Her request had been heard.

Working with creative metaphors

It will be seen that children spontaneously use creative metaphors to cope with their memories of abuse. The importance of these, in the two groups, was that the metaphors provided a way for the children to share their experiences without embarrassment and to create solutions together. The metaphors were not imposed by group but were *joint creations* by the whole group. All the children seemed to be suffering from dissociative episodes in the form of flashbacks or from nightmares or bad dreams. The most natural way to cope with these symptoms of PTSD was by the children co-creating situations with other children or adults. With the precautions and skills of the adults this was done safely without re-traumatization.

The metaphor provides a bridge, 'the space between'. Cox and Theilgaard (1994) suggest that metaphors can influence the unconscious much more than logical language. Creative metaphors regarding risk taking and safety were enacted in the opening active group games. Although these were originally suggested by the staff, the children soon took over this part of the session in both groups and created games which, whilst becoming more risky in some ways, also had many more built-in safety features. For example, in a 'tag' or 'catch' game, 'Mr Wolf' was designated as the catcher and the other children had to 'freeze' if they were caught or tagged. A designated 'safe area' was a pile of floor cushions in the corner, where no one could be caught. However, the children changed the rules so that they carried a large cushion with them and by jumping on this they could create their own 'island of safety'. As one child said, 'You can carry your safe area with you.'

Similarly, the play with the puppets gave the children an opportunity to express feelings in an oblique way. It also gave them a chance to show their most confused feelings. For instance, one boy began to hit another puppet with his own, saying incongruously, 'I am very happy.' One of the girls often appeared confused over gender, picking up ambiguous looking puppets and saying, with frustration, 'It's a man, no, it's a woman, I don't know.' This inability to understand feelings or to express them appropriately is typical of children whose attachment processes have been interrupted or undeveloped. Frequently the children in the groups would say 'I don't know what I feel', but would then tentatively enact feelings through the puppets.

Sometimes it seemed that not only did the children find it difficult to understand their own feelings but also to understand their own identities. In an early session Suzie had drawn a large fish-like creature, after making comments that she herself was 'mean' and 'nasty'. A younger child, Jake, commented that the creature was a 'horrible shark', and Suzie agreed. It may have been her perception of how she felt at the time. Not surprisingly, Suzie sometimes appeared to feel that being too compliant led to abuse so she needed to stress her aggressive, dangerous side.

One of the most moving and creative metaphors was enacted by the younger children in the first group. The group was coming to an end and the children were talking about a party which would be held on the last session. Mark suddenly picked up a pendant from the dressing-up box and put it round his neck, declaring it to be his 'talisman'. Indeed the pendant had played the role of 'protective talisman' in a role play some weeks earlier. The boy also wrapped himself loosely in a long scarf and began a *Riverdance* which was a popular show which had been on the television. He stopped after a few moments and began to bind a female staff member with long scarves so that her movement was very restricted. Without asking, the other children quietly and gently helped him in this task. All co-operated to make sure that no one was harmed. They used up all the scarves and belts which were available and Suzie said to the staff member, 'You are my mother, and you have lost your daughter.'

Mark, the 'Riverdance' boy, said to the 'mother', 'I know where your daughter is, but you will have to wrestle with your conscience before you will find her.' He took over the role of 'conscience', drawing an imaginary circle on the floor around himself. He stood in the pose of a karate fighter. 'Step inside the circle and wrestle with me,' he invited 'mother'. A stylized wrestling match began, with 'mother' still having restricted movement (because of the scarves and belts) and 'conscience' pretending to kick and punch her but withdrawing the blows at the last minute. Suzie, who had cast the staff member in the role of her mother, cried out, 'No, no, stop, I'm here, you have found me, I'm safe!' 'Conscience', however, was relentless. 'Too late,' he cried, 'I'm going to kill her.' Suzie rushed over and grabbed 'mother'. 'I'm rescuing you,' she said.

Quickly Suzie untangled the restrictions around her 'mother' and led her away. In fact her actions reflected exactly Suzie's current relationship with her mother in which she protected her and became 'parentified'. The session was drawing to a close at this point and so the group moved into their usual closure which was always a sharing of feelings about the session and a time to thank people who had been especially helpful. The staff member playing the mother thanked Mark and Suzie who had played the main parts in the above drama (those of 'conscience' and 'daughter'). 'Thank you,' she said, 'for reminding me that I sometimes get things wrong, that I can't be right all the time, but I can be forgiven.' Mark, who had played 'conscience', said, 'My dad used to blame my mum. It wasn't her fault.' By binding the mother in scarves he had recognized the restrictions in which she was placed by the abuser, mother's partner. Suzie, who had played the 'daughter', said, 'My dad hit me and my mum, but then he blamed mum, then he left. It was grandad who hurt me when I was only three. I told my mum.' Mark replied, 'My brother told me not to tell on my dad, but I did. I told my mum. My mum got the blame though.'

The above dramatherapy sessions, spontaneously devised by the children, helped them to look at their experiences through the dramatic mirror. The metaphor provided 'the space between' but the situations were close enough for them to identify with the characters and to empathize with some of them. They illustrated some of the wider dilemmas which are faced by children who are sexually abused. It is clear that relationships with non-abusing parents were deeply damaged and that these mothers were often placed in almost impossible situations as they tried, and sometimes failed, to believe their children against the word of fathers and husbands.

Working with complex post-traumatic stress disorder

It has been noted in Chapter Three that the most common behavioural problems in children who have been sexually abused fit in with a diagnosis of post-traumatic stress disorder (PTSD), and that a more recent update of the criteria for this diagnosis includes particular references to children (American Psychiatric Association 1994). These symptoms include disorganized or agitated behaviour, intrusive recollections (usually expressed in repetitive play), frightening dreams, re-enactment of trauma in flashbacks or in play and intense psychological distress when exposed to cues that resemble the abuse. Some children may have sleep problems, difficulties with anger control, difficulties with concentration and hypervigilance (frozen watchfulness).

Herman (1998) noticed that in situations of prolonged trauma (as in most child sexual abuse, especially intrafamilial) children develop personality changes, including deformations of relatedness and identity. She realized that these symptoms were an extension of PTSD symptoms which are based on combat, disasters and rape, and she called this complex PTSD. If we look at the damage which is caused to developing children by sexual abuse it is clear that the 'symptoms' or effects will be extensive and complex (see Chapter One).

In the groups we noticed that all the children displayed some of the symptoms of complex PTSD. Several of them had transient dissociative episodes in early group sessions, although these had not been mentioned directly by parents and teachers. Several of the children, however, had difficulty in concentrating, both at home and at school, and it may be that the dissociation played a part. They also had other alterations in consciousness as they relived some of their experiences within their play in the groups.

Their coping behaviours often included explosive anger which they sometimes dealt with by projective identification whereby these difficult feelings were projected onto the therapists (Schacht, Kerlinsky and Carlson 1990). Our staff teams were supervised by a group analyst who specialized in child protection work and this helped both teams to cope with the children's projections. Continuing mutually supportive team meetings also helped, coupled with the fact that the projections lessened as the groups progressed.

Other symptoms of PTSD include problems with self-perception, including a sense of helplessness or hopelessness, shame, guilt and self-blame, a sense of defilement or stigma and a sense of complete difference from others. These were strongly shown in all the children at different times. Some of the helplessness, shame and self-blame was shown by their low self-esteem at the start of the group, as demonstrated by the B/G-Steem tests, and by the sociometric test. As I will show in Chapter Seven, these symptoms were considerably reduced by the end of the therapy.

A further group of symptoms which are part of the PTSD model include alterations in relationships with others. This includes the tendency to overplay controlling or victim roles (which, of course, are also coping behaviours). Whilst these roles were being played, in exaggerated and metaphoric ways, within the groups, we did notice a lessening of these symptoms by the end of the groups (see Chapter Seven).

All the children in the groups had unrealistic attributions of total power to the perpetrator, which in itself is another of the symptoms of complex PTSD. Culpability for the crime of sexual abuse and subsequent prosecution is extremely important in child protection in the UK and often overwhelms the more obvious need for counselling or therapy, both for the victims and abusers (Parton and Wattam 1999). Juries are often reluctant to make findings of guilt where the evidence is mostly that of children, even where several children confirm the facts. There is a misunderstanding in the general public about children's abilities to be credible witnesses (see Smith and Woodhead 1999). From the nine children in these two therapy groups, five had testified in court, each with other children who had also been abused. For three children their testimony was not believed and their abusers were found not guilty. For the two children whose case was successful (they were involved in the same case, against several abusers), there was a great deal of supporting photographic evidence. The children who were not believed, therefore, naturally felt that their perpetrators held total power. They continued to find it difficult to accept that they would not be re-abused. Even the two children whose abusers had gone to prison still felt that they would not be protected by the authorities when the men were released.

Phase Three – Resolution

The concept of the third stage of the regenerative model is that children should have begun to redevelop themselves. Obviously, the natural process of child development takes place over at least seven or eight years and this may have been damaged or interrupted at various stages, depending on when the abuse started, how intensive was the trauma, and how long it continued. As we have seen there are also mitigating factors which affect the process, especially the possibilities for functional attachments for children who are being abused by others.

The progress may be reflected in three areas of self-redevelopment:

- ability to understand and express feelings

- awareness of self-identity

- ability to make, maintain or terminate relationships.

It will be seen that during the individual and group work explored in this chapter and in Chapter Five, children appeared to be progressing in their ability and awareness of all three areas. As will be seen in Chapter Eight, the children and their caregivers felt that there had been some changes of behaviour. Our simple tests and exercises also showed some positive results. However, the continuing support and understanding of caregivers is vital if the improvement is to be maintained.

It is sometimes difficult to engage caregivers in therapeutic work with their children. All the families of sexually abused children will have been disrupted and, sometimes, broken irrevocably. Many single parents will be coping with great economic and psychological pressures. All the children in our work had been referred by social services departments to the NSPCC and many of them had other pressures (which are not uncommon in such families). For instance, mothers had severe health problems of their own, and some had lost all family support systems when the abuse was discovered. Several parents had large numbers of children at home and others had children already in the care system. In our work we found that those mothers who had been enabled to seek and receive the support of other women were most able to support their abused children.

Conclusion

There is little doubt that the development of the children in the groups had been damaged by their sexual abuse. During the therapy the children were helped to restart their developmental processes (sometimes by regressing to some extent) and to experiment with new behaviours in a safe situation. Clearly their success in this area was only just beginning and further progress would depend on the support of family and friends and upon further therapy, if that was required, when a different stage of development was reached.

CHAPTER SEVEN

Further Applications of Creative Therapies with Traumatized Children

A global approach

In the earlier part of the 20th century Lev Vygotsky was one of the most brilliant thinkers in Russia. Along with Jean Piaget he was a pioneer in the study of psychology and his unique approach was that *human activity* was the key to development and education (Newman and Holzman 1993). In a country with many different cultures and ethnic groups he recognized that art and literature, poetry and drama, were the means for co-operation and learning. He founded 'special education' for developmentally delayed children. He coined the phrase 'the zone of proximal development' to describe what I have called 'the space between'. This is the space filled with creative activity when two or more people are interacting and learning together. He declared that learning occurs in this co-operative process and this has been my own experience over many years of practical work with traumatized young people.

Since 'new perceptions' are often discovered by different people around the world, it is perhaps not surprising that J.L. Moreno, a near contemporary of Vygotsky, was also making similar discoveries. In his early years he noted the activities of children playing in the parks of Vienna and later, in the USA, he worked in schools and realized that the co-operative links between children themselves, and between them and their teachers, were a vital part of learning. Like Vygotsky he also realized that drama or role playing was a necessary part of that activity. One of Moreno's ideas was that people should be encouraged to try out different roles, as if they were already competent in them.

This is a key component in psychodrama and I have often practised this. A good example is that of an 11-year-old girl who was said to be illiterate, with severe communication problems, whom I mentioned in Chapter Two. She was referred because she had been sexually abused. Although I had been told that she could not write, she was intrigued by the whiteboard in the room and taking the role of 'teacher' she 'wrote' long, mostly incomprehensible sentences on the board. She was encouraged to continue the writing even though most of it was illegible. She managed to communicate with me through this writing, and by acting 'as if' she could write, she gained considerable self-esteem and I was told that her school work began to improve.

Some of the children in schools will, of course, have been sexually and/or physically abused and many more will have suffered emotional abuse. Others may have suffered problems with attachment where parents have parted or through disruption caused by economic reasons. Many of these children exhibit difficulties with learning but it is likely that action methods, which respect joint creativity, can help them. Luxmoore (2002) explains how he uses psychodrama techniques in peer education to assist young people in supporting each other in school. Older students receive some training (sometimes alongside teachers) before they present educative sessions to other young people. The emphasis is on joint action and creativity and Luxmoore quotes a revealing remark from a 17-year-old student who was working with 11–12-year-olds. She said that the children seem to miss 'playtime' (which they had in their junior schools) and implied that they are more open to learning when they are 'in action' together.

She had discovered for herself what Vygotsky and Moreno and later Winnicott (1964), Slade (1995) and many others were stating: children's development and learning are inter-linked. The process begins with the earliest attachments and continues through other relationships, with their peers as well as adults. Curtis (2002), a dance movement therapist, also uses similar methods with children in primary schools who are having difficulties with their education. Jennings and Hickson (2002) use dramatherapy with adolescents whom they describe as 'disaffected youth'. There is plenty of evidence that these methods work and that young people enjoy the opportunity to learn in creative ways.

So creative therapies can be accessed by children of all ages, and by children who have had differing experiences, including traumatization. They are also especially applicable to children with learning difficulties, speech difficulties or those on the autistic spectrum. Smith (2002), a speech and language therapist, uses psychodrama very effectively with her young clients and Gagani and Grieve (2002) work creatively with children with autism. But for children who have suffered sexual abuse, creative therapy may be the *only* way that they are able to communicate what has happened to them and to receive help and repair for the damage they have suffered.

Bacon (2001), acknowledging the importance of the attachment process, links it with secrecy and failure to disclose abuse, especially when the abuse perpetrator is someone within or very close to the family. She understands that children are usually unable to disclose abuse unless they have had some experience of responsive care. I have experienced this many times in my own work. Some of the children whose experiences have been described here in earlier chapters were only able to disclose the abuse because they had some expectation of a positive response. In other words, they had hope that the abuse would stop once they disclosed it. For many children disclosure leads to disbelief and further abuse.

Children have sometimes disclosed sexual abuse to me during creative therapy sessions which have been initiated by social workers who were aware of physical and emotional abuse (but not sexual abuse) by a parent. If the abusive parent has left the home (or been removed) the child may remain with a non-abusive parent. However, the attachment bond with that parent may have been distorted by the presence of the abuser in the home. As we know, sexual abusers may seek to destroy protective attachment bonds with the other parent (Wyre 2000) and so the attachment pattern with that parent is ambivalent or disorganized. If, however, the child has an opportunity to make other attachments which are unconditional in their support, then the child may risk a disclosure to such a supportive figure.

Very young children may demonstrate sexual abuse clearly, with toys or dolls, although the incidents described are usually unconnected iconic memories, as one would expect. Citron (2002) is a psychiatrist and psychodramatist who runs therapeutic groups for very young girls (five to six years old) in her clinic in Stockholm. She describes a little girl who demonstrated, with the use of puppets, how a fox 'kissed the duck in the bottom' several times. The child continued the action by asking for the involvement of the 'secrecy bird' (a puppet handled by a therapist) to whom she related the incident and asked that he tell the police. The 'police', in the form of a monkey puppet handled by another child, took away the fox, to the satisfaction of the little girl. Citron points out that the story could have been a fantasy version of the mother's story of the abuse but this was contradicted by the fact that the child demonstrated, in her re-enactment, how useless it was to say 'no'. This therapist's opinion was that the girl worked directly from her unconscious and was in close contact with her trauma. At a later meeting with the child and her mother, the child had apparently no memory of the enactment she had done in the session. Citron points out that the child was probably dissociating at the moment when she replayed the iconic memory but because the replay was contained within the metaphor of the fox and the duck, and because there was further projection by the use of puppets, it is unlikely that the child was re-traumatized. My opinion is that the child dissociated only for a very short time, at the moment of the recreation of the abuse, but that she was sufficiently in touch with the present to change the story so that it could be repeated to a safe person (the secrecy bird) so that the abuser could be punished (see Chapter Three for other comments on this incident).

Older children may use more elaborate metaphors to demonstrate the abuse they have suffered, as described in the previous chapter. However, because the standard of proof is so high in sexual abuse cases which come before the courts, even an obvious metaphor is unlikely to be acceptable as proof of abuse. Similarly, the evidence of very young children, however explicit, is seldom accepted. The evidence of creative therapists, therefore, may also be unacceptable in the criminal courts, although the Family Court may take a broader approach. Butler-Sloss made it clear in the Cleveland Report (1988) that symbolic or 'fantasy play' may not be acceptable as evidence. I have many examples, however, of children who first 'disclosed' through symbolic play and who then became confident enough to make a full disclosure in an appropriate way (Bannister 1989).

So whether adults using creative therapy are working in a child protection facility, or purely within a therapeutic establishment, they will be under a good deal of pressure from the system. They will also be aware of their own reactions to the horrifying experiences which may be demonstrated in front of them on a daily basis. Their personal experiences and their training will be vital in helping them to cope and to continue to assist distressed children.

Who are the therapists?

Are they especially creative people or just people who are able to access their own creativity and also that of others? It seems to me that it is the latter and that adequate training is essential. A full training in psychodrama takes a minimum of four years and training for dramatherapy or play therapy is at least three years. Other creative therapies (art, music, dance movement) have similar, rigorous training programmes. These are entirely necessary for therapists working with traumatized adults, and even more for those working with vulnerable children. However, Moreno, the inventor of psychodrama, points out that 'creativity and spontaneity affect the very roots of vitality and spiritual development...' (foreword to Blatner 1973, repeated in Blatner 1997). Blatner (1997) also points out that psychodramatic methods have been integrated into many other therapies and into drama in education, personal growth programmes, recovery and self-help groups and many other contexts.

It seems reasonable, therefore, that trained and experienced professionals in other disciplines, who already have much experience in working with traumatized children, can utilize techniques from the creative therapies in their work. During the recent groupwork, described in the previous chapter, I worked alongside such professionals and, working as a supportive team, we were able to generate creativity and spontaneity both within the children and ourselves. Often children and staff are energized by the creativity in individual or group sessions but, on the other hand, both children and staff may complain of tiredness after sessions. It is unwise to expect children to return to school shortly after a session, which is why our sessions were timed to finish at the end of a school day. Such work is undoubtedly stressful to the therapeutic staff and a key component to the success of our project was the regular and skilful supervision sessions provided by our consultant therapist. Such supervision is, of course, quite different from management supervision, and deals with the powerful emotions which are aroused within the therapists as they are exposed to deeply traumatized children.

Many such children have dissociated during the abuse, cutting themselves off from the pain which their bodies experienced. During therapy the practitioners have to take care that the child is not re-traumatized because the child will then automatically dissociate and lose touch with their own body and with the therapist. In the creative play I have described, which stays safely within metaphor and whose boundaries are contained by the therapist, there is little scope for dissociation. However, strong feelings may well be accessed by the child or children and these may be projected on to the therapists (Schacht *et al.* 1990).

Containing these feelings, which may be of anger, despair, guilt or revulsion for instance, may be difficult unless the therapist can share them with other therapists within a team, and with a supervisor. Therapists may introject the feelings and feel guilty that they sometimes feel anger towards the children or despair about their ability to help them. Several of the therapists in our recent groups shared physical feelings of nausea and pain which could be attributed to projected feelings from the children. We all felt relief as we shared these feelings in our supervision sessions. The necessary development of empathy with abused children inevitably leads to personal explorations of our own childhood. Our ability to empathize completely may be dependent on our willingness to explore our own early experiences (which may be similar or different from those of our clients).

Most clinicians of creative therapy have had training which includes such personal exploration and sharing and this may be continued in their own ongoing therapy and supervision. All this provides the safety which is so necessary and important. When working with a team, peer group supervision can be very effective, perhaps with occasional input from another professional. Whatever the method, sharing with colleagues, and having the possibility of ongoing creative personal work, ensures that the therapists remain healthy and able to help their young clients as well as they possibly can.

Different approaches, similar results

As part of my recent research I asked three creative therapists who were working with sexually abused young people for an interview about their work. They may be described as the psychodramatist, the dramatherapist and the play therapist. They were all very experienced and had worked in social work teams, or in hospitals or other clinical and educational settings. The psychodramatist specialized in work with adolescents in groups, and the other two professionals worked, mostly individually, with children from pre-school to teenage years. Most of the children they saw had been diagnosed with behavioural difficulties and the adolescents were inpatients in a psychiatric unit.

I asked all three creative therapists the same series of questions about their work with sexually abused young people. It will be seen that although their individual approaches, and their client groups, were different, their results were similar. As may be expected, those children whose difficulties had been compounded over the years (the adolescents) presented with the most entrenched problems. These young people, as a result of their traumatic experiences, were hospitalized for about a year. Most of the pre-adolescents seen by the dramatherapist were showing disturbed behaviour which was making foster placements difficult. The younger children seen by both the dramatherapist and the play therapist were having problems with their behaviour in school or at home.

Two of the therapists particularly discussed the coping behaviours of the young people. They pointed out that with older children these behaviours had become entrenched and they were always 'either dramatically, one way or the other, controlling or being victimized'. They suggested that this behaviour could only be relinquished by the child if they had the opportunity to create different behaviours and practise them in a safe setting. One therapist, who was also a psychologist, had noticed that abused young people always did badly in a sub-test of an IQ test. This concerned their perception of change (or lack of it) when they were shown two similar pictures. She commented on the 'brain damage' which seemed to have been caused by the abuse.

Her comments are echoed in the work of Glaser (2000) who concludes that chronic abuse and neglect affects the process of brain development. Schore (1997b) also links attachment difficulties to abnormal brain development and a subsequent predisposition to psychiatric disorders. It is, of course, this abnormal brain development which creative therapists seek to reverse. Schore has used attachment theory and the use of PET scans (positron emission tomography) to show that the brain is undoubtedly affected by early abuse. As we have seen, Vygotsky and Moreno, respectively, have endeavoured to show that creative interaction affects the brain in such a way as to enhance learning and also healing. Tests on traumatized (and presumably damaged) children who have undergone such creative, interactive therapy show that their self-esteem and behaviour are improved (see Chapter Eight).

All the therapists in my research were vigorous in their belief that 'empowering' children was the key to self healing. They mentioned the power of simply 'being witnessed', being helped to build their own connected narratives. Some mentioned the repetition of the stages of child development such as projection:

> You can use creative therapies without consciously acknowledging what they [the children] have experienced, which is often too frightening and scary. It helps them to put something into context without initially being verbal, or even admitting to themselves that this is what happened. It helps them to project the experience.

Another commented on embodiment, an early stage of child development: 'They get in touch with their bodies and really begin to feel who they are and what they are capable of.' As may be expected, several therapists remarked on the third stage of child development, role play. A typical comment is: 'As she played her mother she was able to see her point of view for the first time and realise she too was a victim.'

Two of the therapists mentioned that the affinity of the creative therapies to children was based on the fact that they were all connected with play:

> With younger children I believe it is a focused use of play, which they already do. I can see children learning from the play anyway in their homes and in their schools. So it's helping them to focus and then getting some adult acknowledgement. Yes, giving validity to what they are experiencing in life.

> Play helps them to come to terms with the experience, whatever it is, so they do not have to use words. That's a huge advantage for children. It helps to give them a safety mechanism, because of projection. They may want to practise something like assertiveness, they can use puppets for that. That's the advantage of using materials. The sandplay can help them, they can begin to understand the impact of certain actions by

playing them, with figurines. It's like practising before they can fully understand themselves.

It's trauma which inhibits the natural urge to play and to use creative energies. So that need to play has to begin with a creative relationship in some way, in safety.

The therapist who was also an educational psychologist particularly mentioned the advantages of 'learning with all the senses', which occurs in creative therapies: 'Children don't simply learn with their eyes and ears. They can use their bodies and do other things that they can't do in talking therapy.' Some therapists told me what the children themselves had said about the therapy:

When you go [after therapy] you know it's not your fault. When you arrive you think it is.'

I can do things now [which] I couldn't do before.

I can do anything in here. I can be either young or old in here.

I asked all the therapists about the best time to work therapeutically with sexually abused children. As may be expected, they all felt that it was better to begin before coping behaviours had become entrenched, although their experiences had been that most children did not receive help soon enough. Of course, because child sexual abuse does not always leave overtly physical signs (such as bruises), disclosure often depends on the child. The dilemmas and difficulties of this are well documented (Richardson and Bacon 2001). Even in physical abuse children can deny that injuries have been sustained through abuse. If they do not feel safe it may be impossible for children to disclose. As the paediatricians in Cleveland found in 1987, medical evidence can simply be denied.

The therapist working with adolescents in the inpatient facility felt that 12 months of intensive therapy was usually necessary. However, the therapists working with younger children, especially those with supportive parents or carers, felt that short periods of therapy, from six sessions upwards, could be successful. One felt that creative therapies often worked more quickly for children because the metaphors and the use of toys and other props helped them to see a different perspective almost instantly: 'Say that the work was being done in metaphor, using animal toys, she [the child] may say, "How could a kitten or a puppy look after themselves, it isn't their fault.'"

All the therapists agreed that therapy could not begin unless the abuse had stopped and there had been an acknowledgement that it had happened. They also pointed out that therapeutic work should not be carried out with a child unless there was adequate support and therapy for the main carer.

I asked the therapists about the differences in groupwork and individual work. The play therapist only worked with individual children but the other therapists were, in general, very enthusiastic about the power of the group experience, although one therapist warned that they were very stressful on the therapist! She also commented on the importance of assessing each child carefully before a group, to ascertain their developmental damage. She also commented: 'Groups require compromise – from the therapist and probably from the children.' However, both group therapists highlighted the power of the group to move things along quickly, because of the creative interaction between the children themselves. They also mentioned the power of peer support and the reduction of stigma.

When I asked the three therapists a very open question, 'How do you use creative therapies specifically to work with children who have been sexually abused?', they each replied by stressing their particular safety methods and the innate safety of creative therapies. The psychodramatist had been trained in the therapeutic spiral model (Hudgins 2000) where safety in working with survivors of sexual abuse is specifically built in. She stated that she uses transpersonal roles to support the adolescents in her care. For instance, she asks them to choose someone in their life who was not able to support them during the abuse but who could do so in an enactment (perhaps a grandmother or aunt or a mythical figure). One young woman chose a well known singer with a powerful voice to support her. Thus the metaphor of 'a powerful voice' was used (which the abused child did not have) and also the opportunity to use music and voice enabled the protagonist to express herself (when in the role of her own supporter) using her creativity and her body.

This psychodramatist also stressed the formation, for the young people, of 'safe spaces' within the therapy room. Just as the younger children, in the group which I described in Chapter Six, devised safe spaces for their games of 'tag', the adolescents in the psychodrama groups were encouraged to form spaces in the room to which they could retire if they felt unsafe. Several of the young people built 'nests' with the floor cushions and made safety icons or talismans from items in the room. A particular gold scarf was designated as the 'safety scarf' which the young people could wrap around them to signify that they needed to remain secure for the session.

The play therapist felt that the therapeutic space was a safety factor in itself. She stressed the use of projection so that the painful feelings could first be projected into puppets and toys and slowly introjected with the support of the therapist. I was conscious during the interviews with the play therapist and the dramatherapist (both working with younger children) of the similarities in their roles and the role of a 'good enough mother', in Winnicott's terms. These similarities and differences are explored by Grimshaw (1995), who stresses her own personal journey in understanding the significance of this.

Although all the therapists stressed safety, this did not mean that painful feelings were not acknowledged and addressed. The dramatherapist said it was important that painful feelings should be recreated safely: '...to feel the hurt and have it confirmed, not negated as the abuser has done.' However, the psychodramatist, working with adolescents, stressed the importance of practising adult roles. To do this she used the developmental techniques of 'doubling', 'mirroring' and 'role play' frequently. She pointed out that these very damaged young people needed to learn how to express their emotions, to look at the effects of their behaviour on others, and to practise 'standing in the other person's shoes'.

The dramatherapist was particularly interested in the use of touch in therapy and the safety factors concerned in that. She was aware that some therapies forbid touch between therapist and client completely, but she felt (as many creative therapists do) that it may be useful as long as the therapist can be clear about her own motives:

I remember a boy who had experienced a lot of abandonment in his life. I remember the point where he got in touch with his feelings about his mother leaving and he cried bitterly. My first instinct was to put my arms round him but I did not do it, it did not feel right. When I explored it in supervision I knew it was about me having difficulty tolerating his pain...

All the therapists mentioned the necessity for professional supervision as a safety factor in their work. But all of them were clear that the potential for healing lay within the children themselves. The therapists may be able to provide a safe space and to suggest some approaches, but essentially the young people had to discover their own creativity. They had to feel safe enough to interact with the creativity of the therapist and so provide their own solutions and pathway to healing.

I felt that there was no sense of narrowness of approach in any of the therapists. On the contrary, there was always a willingness to embrace diversity (of methods) and to work with others (parents, colleagues, other children in a group) to achieve results. Their wide knowledge of the effects of sexual abuse on children was apparent. They understood that the children's coping behaviours were not necessarily maladaptive but may be effective survival mechanisms (van der Kolk *et al.* 1996). Their understanding of the nature of PTSD and the effects of trauma on child development was also clear. They illustrated the work of Pynoos *et al.* (1996) which shows that children can sometimes have serious learning problems after suffering major trauma. They demonstrated their belief that trauma had changed the children's fundamental awareness and their ability to use words to express feelings.

On analysis of their comments I felt that their objectives could be summarized in four points:

- To enable children to get in touch with their own healing processes.

- To offer children space, distance and safety to look at their difficulties.

- To encourage children to use their own creativity.

- To encourage children to be aware of their bodies as part of the healing process.

The creative therapies, uniquely, offer all these opportunities, especially in the creation of 'the space between', the metaphoric play space (which in itself implies distance), and in the simultaneous recreation of attachment processes.

Dealing with disbelief

For all the therapists involved in my recent research project, and for all the therapists with whom I have worked in teams over many years, the greatest problem may have been dealing with disbelief. It begins in the child protection process, with innocent family members of abused children who have sought explanations of difficult behaviours, but have never considered the possibility of abuse. One such mother, who was now supporting her abused children, spoke of her scepticism when her social worker first told her that her daughter has disclosed sexual abuse by her step-father:

> I was angry. I couldn't believe it. I knew that he knocked me about, that was why I kept leaving home, but he had never been violent with the children. Although he was their step-dad, he had always been a very good dad. He stayed at home while I went to work. They loved him. I thought they wouldn't even miss me when I left.

This mother's self-esteem was very low because of her husband's bullying and violent treatment. She worked long hours in a repetitive job and sometimes stayed with friends overnight instead of returning home. The two older boys were showing behavioural problems at school but it was the seven-year-old girl who told her teacher, and then the social workers, how her father and his friends were sexually abusing her and her brothers. The two boys continued to deny their sister's story, even though there was medical evidence of abuse in all three children. The little girl told how her step-father had threatened to kill them all if they said anything. Having seen his violence towards their mother they had no reason to disbelieve his threat.

The mother's guilt for abandoning her children was immense; her willingness to take total responsibility for the family problems meant that she could not accept what her husband was doing. Like her sons, she continued to deny the possibility until he was taken to court, with his accomplices, and found guilty. With the help of her social worker, and a supportive group of other women who had been physically abused by their partners, her self-esteem rose and she realized how her husband's denigration and abuse of her had probably been part of his plan to abuse the children. Learning the dynamics of sexually abusive behaviour also helped her to recognize many signs of abuse in the children, which she had previously ignored.

When we see that family members, who are intimately involved, can deny that sexual abuse could have occurred, it is perhaps not surprising that a jury in a child sexual abuse trial should also find it difficult to pronounce the defendant 'guilty'. The distress caused to children who are involved in such cases is, of course, immense, as it is to their supportive caregivers. In addition, it is difficult for social workers and therapists to cope with this disbelief when they are convinced of the truth, having been involved with the child protection case, or in pre-trial therapy with the child. Therapists with children are aware that they are unable to maintain 'coaching' (Richardson and Bacon 2001) and that they are no more likely to tell lies than adults. They also understand the difficulties that traumatized children have with expressing themselves. Their anger regarding the verdict may be difficult to contain, especially if the child is still in therapy.

Being in a supportive, therapeutic team atmosphere is probably the best way for practitioners to cope with denial. Having regular input from other professionals, on research findings and new discoveries, also helps to maintain clear thinking. As mentioned, therapeutic supervision is indispensable. An important task for therapists is to look at their own attachments and to see how these have laid a basis for their present attitudes and, especially, their relationships. This brings an understanding of our own attitudes to denial or acceptance of truths, and better equips us to deal with that of others.

Of course, it is not only therapists and family members (including perpetrators) who seek to deny the existence of child sexual abuse. It begins with the child herself who dissociates as she denies what is happening to her body. The denial may continue as she dismisses flashbacks as dreams or 'bad thoughts'. She soon realizes that most caregivers will feed into that denial and may even provide alternative explanations rather than accept the truth, which is unpalatable because it will disrupt family life. The child may be given another, derogatory, label – 'a storyteller' – which follows her into adult life. Some children appear to cope remarkably well with this, until their excessively coping behaviour, whether it is 'over-control' or 'victim-playing', eventually leads them into desperate situations.

As we have seen in this chapter, the older people are before they receive therapy or supportive help, the longer their recovery appears to take. Child protection workers and therapists, together with parents, foster parents and adoptive parents, need to co-operate to ensure that abused children receive the best possible service, at the right time.

CHAPTER EIGHT

Summary of the Regenerative Model

Throughout history philosophers have remarked on the importance of play in human development. They have also commented that play may need to be *refined* to help people to become more aware of life's rewards and difficulties. Most artists will recognize that play is refined in their art, whether it is theatre, visual art, dance, music etc. As we know from primitive cave paintings, from shamanistic practices, and depiction of early musical instruments and dances, mankind has always been aware of artistic processes and their connection with development and healing.

Kaprow (1993), artist and philosopher, suggests that if direct play is denied to adults and gradually discouraged in children, the impulse to play emerges not in true games alone, but in unstated ones of power and deception: 'People find themselves playing less with each other than on or off each other' (p.121). These 'power games' become destructive instead of creative. Their effects on both players are negative, rather than the joint positive effects of playing creatively together. Although some artists prefer to work alone, many, especially in theatre, dance and music, testify to the power of joint creativity.

There is a long history of the use of drama, poetry, art and literature in education. Vygotsky used all of these when he founded 'special education' for developmentally delayed children. He and Piaget engaged in an intellectual debate about the relationship between language and thought in early child development (Vygotsky 1962). Vygotsky was convinced that learning happens in the interface between people in the life space. He stated that children's development occurs first 'between people' and then 'inside the child'. He used the expression 'mind-in-society' (Vygotsky 1978) when explaining that thinking and perceiving are social activities, not individual ones (Newman and Holzman 1993, p.24). There seems to be little doubt that a good teacher is one who can communicate not only the power of the subject to be taught, but a belief in the child's ability to absorb it.

It is significant too that play and artistic pursuits are usually activities which involve the body as well as the mind. Damasio (2000), neurologist and philosopher, stresses the importance of body–mind connections. He suggests that life-regulating devices in the brain regulate the body, creating body-maps, and that the presence of both the brain devices and the body-maps are indispensable for the mechanisms that achieve core consciousness (p.23). He gives a powerful example of a patient who could not remember faces at all. She was shown, randomly, faces of close relatives and friends plus people she had never met. At the same time her skin conductance was recorded with a polygraph, which showed her bodily reactions. Although, because of her total amnesia for faces, she had no idea of the identity of any of the faces, nevertheless virtually every face of a friend or relative generated a distinct skin-conductance response, particularly high with regard to relatives. In other words *her body was remembering what her mind had forgotten.*

Damasio is very clear about the concrete sets of neural patterns which are registered in the brain when we feel emotions. Feelings of joy and pain, which may seem ephemeral, are indelibly recorded and become neural patterns. This gives credence to psychotherapy, which works with such patterns of emotions, and also to the arts which, of course, work directly upon our emotions. There may be nothing ephemeral or transitory about many of our emotions. They become part of our core self. They can be accessed, through arts and through the body, without any conscious application.

When a traumatized person dissociates, her conscious mind is affected by a trigger (often through a bodily response), which affects a pattern of emotions which have been laid down in a traumatic event. Some iconic memories of that traumatic event may also be triggered along with the emotions, and the person re-experiences the event in a flashback. Such experiences may be painful and debilitating, as we have seen in the previous chapters, but it is important not to ignore them. It seems likely that in recreating the events, in symbolic or metaphoric ways and within safe boundaries, fresh neural patterns are registered as the brain responds to the trigger emotions. The original patterns may not be removed, but the brain now has an alternative response when particular emotions are triggered.

In some ways this explanation of dissociation, and of a creative thera-peutic intervention to avoid it, may seem reminiscent of behaviour therapy, which is sometimes used with trauma victims. Behaviour therapy concen-trates on trauma desensitization, exploration of the trauma, and relaxation. It has often been used with soldiers after battle and with victims of sudden disasters, such as terrorist assault. It seems to be very effective in such situa-tions.

But for children who are still developing, who have been abused over long periods by those whom they expected to protect them, it would, of course, be inadequate. Many of these children would have had no support-ive figures around them at the time of the abuse, and would have no experi-ence to evaluate the assaults which were perpetrated against them. Such children, like all children, are physically programmed to develop through continuous interaction, in attachment relationships. They are more likely than adults to be in close touch with their bodies. Adults may often ignore the messages from their bodies, especially if these contradict cognitive messages which they have been given. Children are more familiar with play and with artistic pursuits which may have been discouraged in some adults.

So the regenerative model, which uses child development, attachment theory, creative arts and body consciousness, is more appropriate for young people who have been traumatized. Of course, it is often not just 'what you do' but 'how you do it' that matters and nowhere is this more apparent than in contact with traumatized children. A therapist, a social worker, a parent or anyone who is involved with such children can be sure that their involve-ment will have an impact, so there is a responsibility to make sure that it is a positive one. The negative impact of the child sexual abuser is only too obvious. Just as a rapist may blame his victim because of 'the way she walked' or 'the clothes she was wearing', so a child abuser also blames the child's behaviour and labels normal, childlike behaviour as provocative. This part of the abuse, sometimes called 'grooming', which usually begins at a very early stage before any physical contact, can be most persuasive and debilitating and is the cause of many problems afterwards, as the child struggles to recover.

It follows therefore that the attitudes of other adults and children towards a child who has been abused are crucial in terms of the child's ability to recover from the trauma. Unfortunately, the responses of others, when a child first discloses abuse, are often ambivalent at best. A mother may disbelieve that the abuse has been going on for a long time without being discovered, so her reaction may be 'Why didn't you tell me?', which implies that if it were true, the child would have told. If a child tells a school friend, the reaction may be embarrassed laughter. Children sometimes try to disclose to friends or acquaintances and are greeted by shock and over-reaction, and as a result they quickly retract.

By the time children have gone through the system for disclosure of abuse, and possibly a court case, it is highly likely that their own feelings of guilt and stigma are deeply entrenched. Of course, procedures in such cases are now much improved and many professionals are trained to respond in appropriate ways, but responses from untrained people are bound to compound the children's difficulties. The regenerative model (see Figure 1.1, Chapter One) offers a practical, yet creative way of interacting with children to minimize the damage they have suffered and to recreate a space, and live interaction, where the child's own regenerative powers are given importance and brought into play.

Phase One – Assessment and its importance

Although I have already stressed the importance of assessment before therapy with a sexually abused child, I believe that assessment has another purpose – it can help any professional to understand a child's behaviour. Many people who may not have much experience with sexually abused children may have stereotypical ideas of children's responses. They may assume, for instance, that an aggressive attitude signifies that the child is dealing with the matter in a positive way and does not want involvement by anyone else. The second part of this assumption may be right. The child is heavily into a controlling coping strategy and is afraid that any involvement may demolish this facade. Noting this, as part of the first phase of an assessment, alerts the professional who does not then seek immediately to undermine this behaviour. Understanding why the child is being so controlling and aggressive may help the adult to cope with it. Of course, that is not to say that the adult should become a victim of the child's behaviour, on the contrary; but a calm and rational approach is the first step towards building the important creative relationship.

Similarly, the coping strategy of a child who is quiet and compliant may easily be ignored, both by professionals and by non-abusing caregivers. Such children are extremely vulnerable to further abuse of all kinds, especially as they may gravitate towards very controlling people who will make decisions for them. Such children should be very gently encouraged to make choices and be praised for so doing. They may be difficult to engage but the use of doubling, in particular, can be most helpful.

Assessing a child's attachment relationships also gives us a clue to behaviour. It is only too easy to blame a child's behaviour on inadequate or inappropriate parenting and this causes great distress to parents. It may well be that parents are repeating dysfunctional attachment relationships which they may have made with their own parents (epitomized by the aggressive, physically abusive father who stated that the beatings he received never did him any harm). However, dysfunctional attachment relationships between children and their parents can be changed, as attachment projects in the UK and elsewhere are now proving. This can be done in an atmosphere of no-blame, and children and parents or caregivers can work together in a mutually beneficial way (see Holmes in Bannister and Huntington 2002 and also Chimera *op. cit.*).

Personnel who work in nursery or infant schools can also use a model of assessment which takes the child's development into consideration. Four to five-year-olds who are not yet able to make satisfactory relationships with others are also likely to be stuck in embodiment or projected play. Gentle encouragement to join in simple games where different roles can be played may help such children to develop their understanding of relationships, and sharing. The narrating of stories also helps children to form their own internal narratives and so make sense of what may have been a chaotic early life.

In child protection cases an assessment of the whole child is just as important as an assessment of the physical or sexual abuse which the child has suffered. A medical assessment of the latter may be vital but understanding how development may have been delayed, how attachments may have been distorted, how coping strategies may have affected the child's behaviour are all as important as an assessment of the child's safety. Assessment of safety, of course, involves interviews with caregivers alone and with caregivers and children together. However, social workers need to see children alone, to assess their developmental level. Such an assessment (playing with toys to determine which level of play the child has reached) can easily be done, even if the child and social worker do not speak the same language. Observation of the child with caregivers to assess their attachments is clearly important and, except in the case of infants, much information may also be gathered concerning attachments from the use of sociograms with the child alone. Again, this is a visual exercise and a mutual language is only really necessary for the initial explanation to the child and for the translation of any identifying comments which the child may make, regarding the figurines (see Chapter Five for an explanation of sociograms). It is also necessary to gather information from other contacts with regard to children's usual coping strategies and their ability to protect themselves. The success of future therapy for the child may depend on good assessment at the child protection stage and on the interactive behaviour, with the child, of all the professionals involved.

Of course, a good assessment is not only vital for the success of future therapy. In addition, in the light of recent high-profile serious case reviews where children have died, it is clear that good child protection should always include a thorough assessment process. As a former child protection social worker, I appreciate the pressure and stress of the job, but I still feel that there is no substitute for an interactive, creative session with a child who is suspected of being abused. Listening to the child's voice at this point may be crucial, especially if the child protection worker understands that the child's 'voice' may be heard through the child's body language, facial expressions and behaviour, especially during interaction.

Phase Two – Action and interaction

The core of the regenerative model is, of course, the quality of the attachment with the therapist and the creativity of the action which takes place in the sessions. Total acceptance of the child is probably the most important part of the attachment process, but it must be tempered with firm boundaries so that the child feels safe and protected. It is during this process of building an attachment that the therapist, as well as the child, feels vulnerable. An early agreement on acceptable behaviour must be reached, but many abused children will feel it is necessary to push that agreement to the limit. Testing the boundaries is an important part of the process and flexibility may be the key. Constancy is very important, not just in rules of behaviour, but also in the routine of therapeutic sessions. Using the same room at the same time of day helps with this, as does the availability of the same toys or equipment, even if new equipment is introduced when necessary. If the child is respected, the balance of power between adult and child should be fairly even.

Acting as a witness to the child's story is a very important part of attachment, and of therapy. As children talk about themselves or project their story onto dolls or toy animals, the therapist may reflect or 'mirror' some of the story in words or action, perhaps using figurines or puppets. As children begin to express their feelings (usually through the body at first) the therapist can 'double' the child's body position and verbalize the feeling. Making the body–mind connections, and acknowledging them, prevents dissociation and helps the child to re-experience the stages of development which have been distorted or destroyed by the abuse. Feelings are experienced in the body and, with practice, their connection with the patterns in the brain is understood by the child. Slowly, feelings and identity begin to emerge. The coping behaviours diminish as the child's own personality starts to appear.

Often this process begins within metaphor only and it takes some time before a more literal story can be told. Some children are reluctant to move from symbolic work, especially if they have been sexually abused. This can never be forced and may not even be necessary. Some children can never say what is unspeakable; they may be adults before they have that confidence. Nevertheless, if they can work through their feelings metaphorically and repair some of the developmental damage, the way is clear for them to progress. Their use of the creative arts during this healing play can help them to help themselves in the future. Many artistic adults will acknowledge the therapeutic effect of the work they do.

Phase Three – Resolution and the time factor

Any kind of therapy has to take into consideration the realization that people are ever-changing entities and any changes which they make will be affected by their current circumstances. In abused children this factor is crucial. Because such children have undoubtedly suffered damage to their development, any 'resolution' can only be a step towards their further development. As this proceeds, the young person may need an extraordinary degree of support. An adolescent, for instance, who normally needs from their caregiver a mixture of reassurance and protection plus freedom to experiment, may need to revert to earlier, more childlike behaviour for a while. It is not easy for caregivers to tolerate this, to respond with the physical affection which a younger child would appreciate, and yet to allow the freedom that most adolescents expect.

In my experience, some children who have received therapy which has helped them over their junior school years may need further professional help in adolescence. An alternative suggestion is that their current caregivers are given as much support as necessary, so that *they* can help their children through this difficult time. On the other hand, it may be possible to forestall adolescent problems if early therapy with children is explained to caregivers, at the time, and their own role is supported. Some caregivers (including foster and adoptive parents) may have their own attachment difficulties and some extra professional help may be needed for them.

However, most traumatized children aged over five years who have received sufficient therapy using the regenerative model should have moved forward in the three areas of feelings, identity and relationships. The child should be able to answer her own questions: 'What do I feel?', 'Who am I?' and 'Who are you?'

The child's feelings should be mirrored in her body language so that this is congruent with what she says. Of course we are all familiar with a child (especially an adolescent) who says defiantly 'It's OK. I don't care!' when their body language tells us that they do care. Defending one's feelings against adult interference is perfectly normal. Understanding our own feelings, however, and having the ability to express them if we wish, is a skill which we normally learn in infancy and can re-learn if trauma at that time interrupted our learning.

Once we are aware of our range of feelings then our identity emerges. We are able to make up our own minds (as most healthy two-year-olds demonstrate only too well!) and our character begins to be formed. An awareness of self-identity is often demonstrated in a child receiving therapy when they decide to discard the coping behaviour which they have previously assumed. A self-effacing, victimized child becomes more assertive and a bullying, controlling child becomes more reasonable. Of course, caregivers may be disconcerted when their ten-year-old, formerly submissive and timid child, asserts herself for the first time. Whereas parents can usually manage such behaviour in a two-year-old, the physical capabilities of a much older child can be daunting. Ongoing support for caregivers is clearly necessary.

The final part of self-redevelopment, the ability to make, maintain or terminate relationships, is an obvious extension of the attachment process. A child in therapy may make an attachment to the therapist fairly quickly but it is up to the therapist to ensure that the balance of power is equalized as far as possible within the boundaries which the therapist has laid down. The child must be made aware that the relationship is a temporary one and before the therapy comes to an end it may be helpful for the child to have a visual representation of the number of sessions left, and for this to be discussed appropriately. Ending relationships may be something which an abused child has experienced only too often. Frequently this experience has been so painful that the child has developed a facade of nonchalance. Some children anticipate and circumvent this pain by prematurely ending their own therapy. Exploring the painful nature of ending a relationship, with expressions of feeling on both sides, is a useful part of self-development.

Results of research into the regenerative model

The research which I have carried out on the regenerative model has, of course, been qualitative as the previous chapters show, but when the research groups were run there were some quantitative tests done, mainly as part of assessment. To measure self-esteem and to determine the locus of control in the children, before and after therapy, they were asked to fill in a simple yes/no form which asked about their views of themselves (Maines and Robinson 1988). In addition, their parents/carers were asked to fill in behavioural assessment forms before and after the groups. For the pilot group the Devereux test (Naglieri, Le Buffe and Pfeiffer 1993) was used. However, this assessment (often used in educational settings) tends to concentrate on problems and negative feelings and does not give a rounded view of the child. When discussing this assessment with caregivers the professionals found that there was no encouragement for exploration of positive traits and feelings in the child. This did not promote good relationships, either with parents or between parents and their children, so for the main group a test was used which asked about positive as well as negative behaviour: the strengths and difficulties questionnaire (Goodman 1997). This latter test also considered the views of teachers as well as parents and this helped to give an even fuller picture of the child.

The main assessment indicator, however, and an indicator of change in behaviour post-therapy, was the Morenian sociometric test which has been described in Chapter Five. Photographs of some of these sociograms appear below, together with a discussion of their significance. A summary of the more formal tests is also given here.

Self-esteem and locus of control tests

The self-esteem of all the children improved somewhat after the groups. On average their score was increased by 2.4 per cent and the range lay between 1 and 5 per cent. Their maladaptive coping behaviours were considerably decreased. This was shown by the locus of control test which showed 50 per cent of the children reverting to 'normal' behaviour and the other half showing a lessening of their controlling or victimized behaviours.

Behavioural assessment forms

As mentioned above, it was felt that the Goodman scale, used in the main group, made a broader assessment of behaviour because positive as well as negative behaviours were assessed and, in addition to caregivers, teachers were also consulted. The Devereux test depended a great deal on the relationship between the caregiver and the child and this was, of course, likely to be affected by the caregiver's own difficulties and by the quality of their own parenting. A good example of this was one parent who assessed the child's behaviour as 'much improved' in the area of self-protection, but who was much less happy with the child's general improvement in self-assertiveness. This was, of course, more difficult for the parent to understand and to cope with.

However, 100 per cent of the adults consulted felt that there was an improvement in most areas of behaviour, especially in self-protection. It was most helpful to obtain the views of the teachers who confirmed that behaviour had improved, although in a couple of children there was still 'room for further improvement'. Both these children had suffered other traumatic events in addition to the trauma of sexual abuse. We were, of course, well aware that some children needed further support after the groups and, indeed, one continued to be seen by myself and others were referred back to social workers.

Sociometric tests

As I have explained in Chapter Five, I have adapted Moreno's sociometric test for my work with children. His idea was that people should be encouraged to look at attraction and repulsion to others, either in their work groups or social groupings. The social atom, or network, of a person is defined by the attraction or repulsion felt towards others and this feeling is named by Moreno as 'tele'. It is usually a two-way process which signifies the positive or negative feelings between two people and also the importance or strength of those feelings. Moreno first used the test in schools where teachers found that children's learning was increased when they were allowed to sit in groups where there was mutual compatibility. In his experiments the children were asked to move themselves into such constellations until they felt comfortable.

In my adaptation for individual work with children I found that they seem to have no difficulties in completing such a test when it is projected, in miniature, onto small figurines. They choose figurines to represent themselves and their social circle and they easily incorporate people who have died or moved away, and they often include pets. I usually make a comment such as: 'Choose people who are important in your life, whether you think they are good or bad.' I may say: 'Show me how close they are to you.' Sometimes they add scenery, such as caves or fences, although this is always left to the spontaneity of each child.

Children may also be given the choice of drawing their sociogram instead of using the small figures. This usually works just as well. Of course, this test may also be used with adults who often prefer to use diagrams. This is a simple way for adults to consider their own situations but the three-dimensional aspect of the figures, which includes the significance of each chosen figure, may be more revealing.

All the children in the groups showed significant changes in their before and after sociograms, but perhaps two examples will serve to illustrate the kind of differences which were typical of all the children. A nine-year-old boy (and his younger brother) had been abused by an uncle who continued to deny the abuse. Some members of his wider family were also supporting the abuser and proclaiming this man's innocence. The boy's immediate family believed him and his brother, but the jury had returned a 'not guilty' verdict.

His first sociogram (done at assessment) showed himself and his immediate family and several members of his extended family all represented by 'people' figurines, huddled closely behind a long toy fence (which he put in place even before he placed the figurines). He did not speak as he arranged the figurines but merely pushed them close together. Menacing them from the other side of the fence are three figures: a large black spider in the centre, flanked by two green insect monsters (see Figure 8.1). The boy did not explain who was represented by the insects, and it felt inappropriate to ask at the time. However, it seemed probable that the spider was his abuser and the other two were the abuser's chief protectors in his family.

Figure 8.1 Sociogram: boy – before group therapy

His second sociogram, six months later after the group, showed several differences (see Figure 8.2). He and his family were represented not only by people figures but also by larger, friendly but protective looking animal figures, such as a lion and two large hedgehogs and two horses. The boy named the lion as himself and a 'hero' figure, slightly behind him as a supporter, 'Uncle Dan'. The fence has disappeared and so have the two 'insect' henchmen (or women). Instead the spider stands alone looking rather forlorn, at some distance behind the family group (not in their vision). This time the boy named the spider as his abuser and stated that he could not wipe out what had happened but he had put it behind him. He had the choice of a large number of figures and had no access to his previous sociogram but probably remembered choosing the spider from before.

Figure 8.2 Sociogram: boy – after group therapy

Another child in the group, a nine-year-old girl, used a rather small number of figurines in her first sociogram (see Figure 8.3). She chose an ambiguous squishy pink lizard for herself and seemed to have no supportive figures close to her, except for two school friends and her dog. Her mother was a floppy pink spider, some distance away. Figures wearing doctors' white coats hovered near the periphery of the group, together with a fairy queen and a bear. She named these as supportive teachers. Her abusive brother was a large rabbit who was furthest away from her, next to a younger brother.

Figure 8.3 Sociogram: girl – before group therapy

Figure 8.4 Sociogram: girl – after group therapy

Six months later her sociogram showed great changes (see Figure 8.4). Her mother (who had been receiving support from another NSPCC group) now appeared closest to her, and was now in the guise of Wonder Woman. Her father was also nearby but he had assumed the role of the floppy pink spider.

Her abusing brother was now represented by the small pink squishy lizard, which she had formerly chosen for herself. I wondered if she had now stopped blaming herself for the abuse and had been able to understand her brother's role in the incidents. She chose an ordinary looking girl figure for herself so perhaps she felt that some of the stigma of abuse had disappeared. Her abusing brother was closer to her but her best friend seemed still protective, between him and her.

The changes in both sociograms could be explained to some extent by the passage of time and changes in the family. For instance, the girl's mother was now able to support her much more. Little had changed in the boy's extended family except that Uncle Dan had chosen to believe him instead of the rest of the extended family. However, the boy's understanding of events seemed to have changed considerably and he had fitted the events into his narrative memory. The girl also seemed to show a major change in her perception in that she was no longer carrying the guilt for the events. It seems likely therefore that these children would be unlikely to suffer from dissociation when stimulated by reminders of the abuse. They showed in the sociograms that they were now able to interact much better in relationships and this may indicate that the third stage in their development had been completed.

Observations made during the groups

During the groups all the children demonstrated their improvement in the areas of self-redevelopment, as listed in Phase Three of the model. Not only were relationships enhanced as mentioned above but the two earlier stages, of understanding and expressing feelings, and having an awareness of self-identity, were practised and demonstrated. With the use of doubling and mirroring during the groups, they had learnt what their bodies were expressing. By using puppets and projection through art (drawing and clay modelling) they demonstrated that they had become more aware of their identity.

There were, of course, still many areas which the children were exploring. For instance, one girl, now approaching puberty, who had also suffered the loss of her mother during her early years, appeared to have some gender identity difficulties, as mentioned in earlier chapters. This could have many explanations. It may be part of normal adolescent restructuring, it could indicate the possibility of a normal but different sexual orientation, it could also indicate that she had not fully relinquished her coping behaviours after the abuse and that she saw masculine behaviour (which she defined as aggressive) as a protective shield. It is possible that, after a period of adjustment following the group, she would become less conflicted and would accept herself, whatever her orientation.

On the other hand she may need further therapeutic support as she goes through adolescence. It is possible that the experience of losing her mother during her early development made her more vulnerable to later abuse by a neighbour, who abused a number of similarly vulnerable children (including her older sister). This experience compounded her feelings of powerlessness which she sought to overcome by an aggressive attitude. As we work with sexually abused children it is always important to remember that they are whole people, in every sense of the word, and that the abuse may be only a small part of their experience. The extent of trauma which it causes may depend on many other aspects of the child's life. As I have stated, some children (such as this girl's older sister) may be less affected by the abuse because of their own stage of development. Others may be less affected because this trauma is not compounded by other, earlier trauma. Others may cope much better because of the way in which their trauma was discovered and the way they were supported when it was.

Comments of children and families

All the children were interviewed with their parents/carers after the group and they were all very positive about their time in the group. Typical comments from the children were: 'I've started to get better and I don't have nightmares now' (girl, 10); 'The group was fun and I'm glad I came' (boy, 8); 'I can sort things out myself now, and the group helped' (girl, 9); 'I miss my friends in the group, I'm sorry it finished' (girl, 11).

Comments from caregivers included: 'The group was a big help, I've noticed a change in…'; 'She is looking so much better now, after the group'; 'He is coming out of himself, he's got more friends now, more confident'; 'The group was magnificent, she stands up for herself now, no problem.'

Conclusions

The model which I have illustrated is based upon the work of many theorists and practitioners, particularly in the field of child protection. It is a combination of tacit knowledge, the knowledge which may have to be experienced to be understood, and of theoretical knowledge (Fook 2002). Its eclecticism may be one of its strengths because it does not rely on one or two theorists but includes the work of many people who have observed young people in natural settings for many years. In particular, it draws upon my own extensive practice with young people who have suffered trauma of many kinds, including the trauma of sexual abuse. I would say that my main theoretical inspiration has been from Moreno, who began his thoughts on psychodrama by observing children at play. The observations of Bowlby and Winnicott, which I revisited during the research, have also been essential in the formation of the model. My main practical inspiration, however, has been the children with whom I have been privileged to work, especially within the research, and the experienced colleagues with whom I have shared practice.

The model is a practical one which allows plenty of room for practitioners to develop their own idiosyncratic ways of working. Naturally, it also allows for the differences in individual children. I have worked cross-culturally with children, and alongside colleagues from different cultures. Although cross-cultural work is possible, and may be necessary for some children where practitioners of similar cultures cannot be found, it is important that therapists and children have a good understanding of each other's culture. For instance, attachments between children and their carers may be multiple and of a different order in some cultures and this must be borne in mind, at assessment particularly.

Practitioners who are not aware of the stories and myths of a culture other than their own may have difficulty in relating to a child through these media. However, many stories (such as *Cinderella* or *Beauty and the Beast*) are told in different forms throughout the world (see Warner 1994 for a good discussion of this). Recently in Sweden, I discovered that the nursery story *The Three Little Pigs* (mentioned in previous chapters) was as well known there as in the UK. With many children, however, it is the popular culture of the day, dispersed through television and popular music, which provides a mutual background from which to work. This necessitates an attitude of keeping in touch with popular culture and I have been grateful to my own children and grandchildren in this regard.

The model may also be adapted for use with disabled children, that is children who suffer prejudice and discrimination because of perceived functional limitations. My own experience in this area has mostly been with children with learning difficulties, for which the model is quite appropriate. Adaptations would have to be made with children with physical difficulties, but since it is always important to adapt the model according to each child or group, this should not present problems. Differences here would probably centre around the kind of creative play or arts which would be possible or most appropriate, and since the creativity of the therapist and child is all important in this approach, their joint creativity should solve this.

One of the most elusive areas of understanding in this work is knowing when a child is ready and able to respond to therapy. I have illustrated the fact that children cannot respond when they do not feel safe within their intimate environment, nor when they feel unsafe in the therapy itself, but it is my experience that rather than simply an absence of danger there has to be also a more positive environment for the child. We need to remember that no therapist heals a child: children heal themselves, but they can be helped to get in touch with their own healing mechanisms. Children who are supported and affirmed by understanding carers, or family and friends and teachers, respond more quickly and make greater progress than those who are still busy protecting others within their homes, or are fighting prejudice and misunderstanding in their environment.

The regenerative model returns the power of regeneration to the young person. It merely seeks to facilitate the process whereby children who may have been disempowered time after time can gain the will, the strength and the creativity to reclaim their lives.

The future

The importance of working therapeutically with abused children, especially those who have been sexually abused in early childhood by caregivers, has been illustrated in this work. It seems clear that early intervention, to rebuild attachment processes, is necessary for the psychological well being of each child. It seems likely that such interventions may stimulate right brain activity which will then enable the young person to develop more fully.

These processes will then, of course, affect the next generation of children, since their parents may be able to care for them in more positive ways.

I have discussed coping behaviours, in which abused children may either demonstrate their victimization by being extremely compliant and subdued, or they may identify with the abuser and become very controlling and abusive themselves. Most children are only able to dispense with these coping behaviours when they have resolved their traumatic experiences and moved forward in their development. This may mean, of course, that some children who are coping by being controlling and aggressive will sexually abuse other children. Such behaviour cannot, of course, be ignored. Treatment for adolescents who sexually abuse is discussed by O'Callaghan and Print (1994). They point out that the majority of the victims of abusing adolescents are children much younger than themselves. Access to such children is often obtained by siblings or other relatives during babysitting. So very young children may be abused by temporary carers, as well as by permanent caregivers, and an abusive cycle may be further perpetuated.

The abusive behaviour of these young people must be treated in the most effective way, usually by helping them to control their behaviour. O'Callaghan and Print state:

> There is an acceptance that adolescent sex abusers have developed a dysfunctional behaviour which is not generally mitigated by time alone. The deviant behaviours and thinking processes of the abusers originate from negative experiences, such as various forms of abuse in childhood, which lead to the abuser developing deep needs for power, acceptance and aggression which they meet through abusive sexual behaviour. (p.156)

Their 'negative experiences', of course, may be physical, sexual or emotional abuse and may also include experiences where the young people have been witnesses to domestic violence and abuse in which they were not direct victims.

Behaviour control programmes then are very necessary for young people whose abusive behaviour has become entrenched, where it is reinforced through masturbation, and where families are unsupportive or unable to protect other victimized children. However, one of the key factors in most rehabilitation work with offenders, especially sexual offenders, is often 'victim empathy'. This helps the offender to role reverse with their victim so that they can understand and identify with the feelings of victimization. If we assume that most sexual offenders have had their early development damaged because they have suffered some kind of abuse or neglect, we know that the offender may not be able to regulate his own emotions (because of attachment problems), may have little sense of his own identity, and may be quite unable to understand the feelings of another person. He cannot answer the questions 'What do I feel?', 'Who am I?' and 'Who are you?'. Working with victim empathy then may be impossible or very difficult for some, maybe the majority of, offenders. I have worked with many adolescents and adults who have, initially, been unable to role reverse in an effective way.

It makes sense therefore that young offenders should be offered parallel treatment programmes. In addition to a programme which helps them to regulate their offending behaviour they should be offered creative therapy on the lines of the regenerative model. This will help them to heal themselves and to develop their emotional control, their sense of identity and their role repertoire, especially their empathy with others. It may be that programmes such as that described by O'Callaghan and Print (*op. cit.*) already provide many of these elements since they speak of using 'action techniques, such as sculpting, doubling and role-play'. Role play is also used in cognitive behavioural treatment of sex offenders (see Beckett 1994), often to help offenders to hear their own cognitive distortions.

Predictably, after high-profile child sexual abuse cases, which almost always concern abduction and/or murder, the public reacts with anger and fear towards those whom they term 'paedophiles'. This term is seen as an indication of their mental illness (at best) or of their irrevocable wickedness. It is true that programmes for adult sexual offenders may have limited success, especially in prisons when attendance is dependent on the co-operation of the prison system. Although these programmes should be increased and supported, it is more important for the future that young people receive help before deviant behaviour becomes established. Their non-abusing parents need more support in understanding and assisting their children and the young people themselves need early therapeutic intervention if society is serious about tackling child abuse.

References

Adams-Tucker, C. (1981) 'A socioclinical overview of 28 sex-abused children.' *Child Abuse and Neglect 5*, 361–367.

Adams-Tucker, C. (1982) 'Proximate effects of sexual abuse in childhood: A report on 28 children.' *American Journal of Psychiatry 139*, 1252–1256.

Ageton, S. (1983) *Sexual Assault among Adolescents: Part II, The Adolescent Victim.* Toronto, Ont: Lexington.

Ainsworth, M.D.S. (1969) 'Object relations, dependency and attachment: A theoretical review of the infant–mother relationship.' *Child Development 40*, 969–1025.

Ainsworth, M.D.S., Blehar, M., Aters, E. and Wall, S. (1978) *Patterns of Attachment: A Psychological Study of the Strange Situation.* Hillsdale, NJ: Erlbaum.

American Psychiatric Association (1987) *Diagnostic and Statistical Manual of Mental Disorders (DSM-III-R).* Washington, DC: American Psychiatric Association.

American Psychiatric Association (1994) *Diagnostic and Statistical Manual of Mental Disorders (DSM-IV).* Washington, DC: American Psychiatric Association.

Axline, V.M. (1947; reprinted 1969) *Play Therapy.* New York: Ballantine Books.

Axline, V.M. (1969) *Play Therapy* (2nd edn). New York: Ballantine Books.

Bach-y-Rita, P. (1990) 'Brain plasticity as a basis for recovery of function in humans.' *Neuro-psychologia 28*, 547–554.

Bacon, H. (2001) 'Attachment, trauma and child sexual abuse: An exploration.' In S. Richardson and H. Bacon (eds) *Creative Responses to Child Sexual Abuse: Challenges and Dilemmas.* London: Jessica Kingsley Publishers.

Bagley, C. (1996) 'A typology of child sexual abuse: Addressing the paradox of interlocking emotional, physical and sexual abuse as causes of adult psychiatric sequels in women.' In C. Bagley (ed) *Children, Sex and Social Policy.* Aldershot: Avebury.

Bagley, C. and Thurston, W.E. (1996) *Understanding and Preventing Child Sexual Abuse, Vol. 2.* Aldershot: Arena.

Bagley, C. and Young, L. (1990) 'Depression and suicidal behaviours as sequels to sexual abuse in childhood.' In M. Rothery and G. Cameron (eds) *Child Maltreatment: Expanding our Concepts of Helping.* Hillsdale, NJ: Erlbaum.

Bagley, C. and Young, L. (1995) 'Juvenile prostitution and child sexual abuse: A controlled study.' In C. Bagley (ed) *Child Sexual Abuse and Mental Health in Adolescents and Adults: Canadian and British Perspectives.* Aldershot: Avebury.

Bannister, A. (1989) 'Healing action.' In C. Wattam, J. Hughes and H. Blagg (eds) *Child Sexual Abuse: Listening, Hearing and Validating the Experiences of Children.* London: Longman/NSPCC.

Bannister, A. (1990; reprinted 1998) *From Hearing to Healing: Working with the Aftermath of Child Sexual Abuse.* Chichester: John Wiley/NSPCC.

Bannister, A. (1991) 'Learning to live again.' In P. Holmes and M. Karp (eds) *Psychodrama: Inspiration and Technique.* London: Routledge.

Bannister, A. (1995) 'Images and action.' In S. Jennings (ed) *Dramatherapy with Children and Adolescents.* London: Routledge.

Bannister, A. (1997) *The Healing Drama: Psychodrama and Dramatherapy with Abused Children.* London: Free Association Books.

Bannister, A. (2000) 'Prisoners of the family: Psychodrama with abused children.' In P.F. Kellermann and M.K. Hudgins (eds) *Psychodrama with Trauma Survivors.* London: Jessica Kingsley Publishers.

Bannister, A. and Huntington, A. (eds) (2002) *Communicating with Children and Adolescents: Action for Change.* London: Jessica Kingsley Publishers.

Bannister, A. and Prodgers, A. (1983) 'Psychodrama in cases of child abuse.' *Journal of Dramatherapy 7,* 1, 23–26.

Beckett, R. (1994) 'Assessment of sex offenders.' In T. Morrison, M. Erooga and R.C. Beckett (eds) *Sexual Offending against Children: Assessment and Treatment of Male Abusers.* London and New York: Routledge.

Bender, L. and Woltman, A.G. (1936) 'The use of puppet shows as a psychotherapeutic measure for behavior problem children.' *American Journal of Orthopsychiatry 6,* 341–354.

Bender, L. and Woltman, A.G. (1937) 'Puppetry as a psychotherapeutic measure with problem children.' *New York State Association of Occupational Therapists 7,* 1–7.

Benward, J. and Densen-Gerber, J. (1975) 'Incest as a causative factor in anti-social behaviour: An exploratory study.' *Contemporary Drug Problems 4,* 323–340.

Bettelheim, B. (1976; reprinted 1991) *The Uses of Enchantment.* London: Penguin.

Bifulco, A., Brown, G.W. and Harris, T.O. (1994) 'Childhood experience of care and abuse (CECA): A retrospective interview measure.' *Journal of Child Psychology and Psychiatry 35,* 8, 1419–1435.

Blatner, H. (1973) *Acting-In: Practical Applications of Psychodramatic Methods.* New York: Springer.

Blatner, A. (1997) *Acting-In: Practical Applications of Psychodramatic Methods* (3rd edn). New York: Springer.

Bolen, R.M., Russell, D.E.H. and Scannapieco, M. (2000) 'Child sexual abuse prevalence: A review and re-analysis of relevant studies.' In C. Itzin (ed) *Home Truths About Child Sexual Abuse: Influencing Policy and Practice.* London: Routledge.

Bowlby, J. (1953) *Child Care and the Growth of Love.* Harmondsworth: Pelican Books.

Bowlby, J. (1969) *Attachment and Loss: Vol. 1 Attachment.* London: Tavistock.

Briere, J. (1984) 'The effects of childhood sexual abuse on later psychological functioning: Defining a post-sexual abuse syndrome.' Paper presented at the Third National Conference on Sexual Victimisation of Children, Washington, DC.

Briere, J. and Runtz, M. (1986) 'Suicidal thoughts and behaviours in former sexual abuse victims.' *Canadian Journal of Behavioural Science 18,* 413–423.

Briere, J. and Runtz, M. (1988) 'Post sexual abuse trauma.' In G.E. Wyatt and G.J. Powell (eds) *Lasting Effects of Child Sexual Abuse.* London: Sage.

Briere, J., Evans, D., Runtz, M. and Wall, T. (1988) 'Symptomology in men who were molested as children: A comparison study.' *American Journal of Orthopsychiatry 58*, 457–461.

Bronfenbrenner, U. (1979) *The Ecology of Human Development.* Cambridge, MA: Harvard University Press.

Burgess, A.W., Hartman, C.R. and McCormack, A. (1987) 'Abused to abuser: Antecedents of socially deviant behaviours.' *American Journal of Psychiatry 144*, 1, 431–436.

Burr, V. (1995) *An Introduction to Social Constructionism.* London: Routledge.

Butler-Sloss, Rt Hon Justice E. (1988) *Report of the Inquiry into Child Abuse in Cleveland 1987.* London: HMSO.

Cairns, K. (1999) *Surviving Paedophilia.* Stoke on Trent: Trentham Books.

Carbonell, D.M. and Parteleno-Barehmi, C. (1999) 'Psychodrama groups for girls coping with trauma.' *International Journal of Group Psychotherapy 49*, 3, 285–306.

Cattanach, A. (1992) *Play Therapy with Abused Children.* London: Jessica Kingsley Publishers.

Cattanach, A. (1997) *Children's Stories in Play Therapy.* London: Jessica Kingsley Publishers.

Cawson, P. (2002) *Child Maltreatment in the Family: The Experience of a National Sample of Young People.* London: NSPCC.

Chesner, A. (2002) 'Playback theatre and group communication.' In A. Chesner and H. Hahn (eds) *Creative Advances in Groupwork.* London: Jessica Kingsley Publishers.

Chimera, C. (2002) 'The yellow brick road.' In A. Bannister and A. Huntington (eds) *Communicating with Children and Adolescents: Action for Change.* London: Jessica Kingsley Publishers.

Citron, C. (2002) 'Touch me – No! Creative therapies with young sexually abused children.' In A. Bannister and A. Huntington (eds) *Communicating with Children and Adolescents: Action for Change.* London: Jessica Kingsley Publishers.

Colton, M. and Vanstone, M. (1996) *Betrayal of Trust.* London: Free Association Books.

Constantine, L.L. (1980) 'Effects of early sexual experiences: A review and synthesis of research.' In L.L. Constantine and F.M. Martinson (eds) *Children and Sex: New Findings, New Perspectives.* Boston: Little, Brown.

Conte, J.R. and Schuerman, J.R. (1988) 'The effects of sexual abuse on children.' In G.E. Wyatt and G.J. Powell (eds) *Lasting Effects of Child Sexual Abuse.* London: Sage.

Cox, M. and Theilgaard, A. (1987) *Mutative Metaphors in Psychotherapy: The Aeolian Mode.* London: Tavistock.

Curtis, S. (2002) 'Providing dance movement therapy within a mainstream school.' In A. Bannister and A. Huntington (eds) *Communicating with Children and Adolescents: Action for Change.* London: Jessica Kingsley Publishers.

Damasio, A. (2000) *The Feeling of What Happens: Body, Emotion and the Making of Consciousness.* London: Vintage.

Dixen, J. and Jenkins, J.O. (1981) 'Incestuous child sexual abuse: A review of treatment strategies.' *Clinical Psychology Review*, 1, 211–222.

Doran, C. and Brannan, C. (1996) 'Institutional abuse.' In P. Bibby (ed) *Organised Abuse*. Aldershot: Arena.

Eichenbaum, L. and Orbach, S. (1982) *Outside In, Inside Out, Women's Psychology: A Feminist Psychoanalytic Approach*. Harmondsworth: Pelican.

Emunah, R. (1995) 'From adolescent trauma to adolescent drama: Group drama therapy with emotionally disturbed youth.' In S. Jennings (ed) *Dramatherapy with Children and Adolescents*. London: Routledge.

Erikson, E. (1950) *Childhood and Society*. New York: Norton (reprinted 1977, Paladin).

Fahlberg, V. (1994) *A Child's Journey through Placement*. London: BAAF.

Farmer, C. (1998) 'The psychodramatic treatment of depression.' In M. Karp, P. Holmes and K. Bradshaw-Tauvon *The Handbook of Psychodrama*. London and New York: Routledge.

Ferenzi, S. (1955) *Confusion of Tongues between Adults and the Child in Final Contributions to the Problems and Methods of Psychoanalysis*. New York: Basic Books.

Finkelhor, D. (1984) *Child Sexual Abuse: New Theory and Research*. New York: Free Press.

Finkelhor, D. (1994) 'Current Information on the scope and nature of child sexual abuse: The future of children.' *Sexual Abuse of Children 4, 2*, 31–53.

Finkelhor, D., Hotaling, G., Lewis, L. and Smith, G. (1989) 'Sexual abuse and its relationship to later sexual satisfaction, marital status, religion and attitudes.' *Journal of Interpersonal Violence 4*, 379–399.

Fook, J. (2002) 'Theorizing from practice: Towards an inclusive approach for social work research.' *Qualitative Social Work 1*, 1, 79–95.

Fox, J. (1987) *The Essential Moreno*. New York: Springer.

Friedrich, W.N. (1988) 'Behaviour problems in sexually abused children.' In G.E. Wyatt and G.J. Powell (eds) *Lasting Effects of Child Sexual Abuse*. London: Sage.

Friedrich, W.N. (1995) *Psychotherapy with Sexually Abused Boys*. Thousand Oaks, CA: Sage.

Gagani, E. and Grieve, S. (2002) 'Let's make a bridge: Working in action with autistic children.' In A. Bannister and A. Huntington (eds) *Communicating with Children and Adolescents: Action for Change*. London: Jessica Kingsley Publishers.

Gagnon, J. (1965) 'Female child victims of sex offenses.' *Social Problems 13*, 176–192.

Gelinas, D.J. (1983) 'The persisting negative effects of incest.' *Psychiatry 46*, 312–332.

Gersie, A. (1987) 'Dramatherapy and play.' In S. Jennings (ed) *Dramatherapy: Theory and Practice for Teachers and Clinicians*. London: Croom Helm.

Gersie, A. (1992) *Earthtales*. London: Greenprint (Merlin Press).

Glaser, D. (2000) 'Child abuse and neglect and the brain – A review.' *Journal of Child Psychology and Psychiatry 41*, 1, 97–116.

Goodman, R. (1997) 'The strengths and difficulties questionnaire: A research note.' *Journal of Child Psychology and Psychiatry, 38*, 5, 581–586.

Grimshaw, D. (1995) 'Shall I be mother? The development of the role of the dramatherapist and reflections on transference/counter-transference.' In S. Jennings (ed) *Dramatherapy with Children and Adolescents*. London: Routledge.

Herman, J.L. (1981) *Father–Daughter Incest*. Cambridge, MA: Harvard University Press.

Herman, J.L. (1992; reprinted 1998) *Trauma and Recovery: From Domestic Abuse to Political Terror.* London: Pandora.

Herman, J.L. and Hirschman, L. (1977) 'Father–daughter incest.' *Signs 1*, 1–22.

Herman, J.L. and van der Kolk, B.A. (1987) 'Traumatic antecedents of borderline personality disorder.' In B.A. van der Kolk (ed) *Psychological Trauma.* Washington, DC: American Psychiatric Press.

Holmes, P. (1992) *The Inner World Outside: Object Relations Theory and Psychodrama.* London: Routledge.

Holmes, P. (2002) 'The use of action methods in the treatment of the attachment difficulties of long-term fostered and adopted children.' In A. Bannister and A. Huntington (eds) *Communicating with Children and Adolescents: Action for Change.* London: Jessica Kingsley Publishers.

Holmes, P. and Karp, M. (eds) (1991) *Psychodrama: Inspiration and Technique.* London: Routledge.

Horwath, J. (ed) (2000) *The Child's World: Assessing Children in Need.* London: Department of Health/NSPCC/University of Sheffield.

Howe, D. (1993) *On Being a Client.* London: Sage.

Howe, D. (1995) *Attachment Theory for Social Work Practice.* Basingstoke: MacMillan.

Howe, D. (2000) 'Attachment.' In J. Horwath (ed) *The Child's World: Assessing Children in Need.* London: Department of Health/NSPCC/Sheffield University.

Hudgins, M.K. (1998) 'Experiential psychodrama with sexual trauma.' In L.S. Greenberg, G. Lietaer and J.C. Watson (eds) *Handbook of Experiential Psychotherapy.* New York: Guilford Press.

Hudgins, M.K. (2000) 'The therapeutic spiral model: Treating PTSD in action.' In P.F. Kellermann and M.K. Hudgins (eds) *Psychodrama with Trauma Survivors.* London: Jessica Kingsley Publishers.

Hudgins, M.K. and Drucker, K. (1998) 'The containing double as part of the Therapeutic Spiral Model for treating trauma survivors.' *The International Journal of Action Methods 51*, 63–74.

Hudgins, M.K., Drucker, K. and Metcalf, K. (2000) 'The containing double: A clinically effective psychodrama intervention for PTSD.' *The British Journal of Psychodrama and Sociodrama 15*, 1, 58–77.

Itzin, C. (2000) *Home Truths about Child Sexual Abuse: Influencing Policy and Practice. A Reader.* London: Routledge.

Janet, P. (1919) *Psychological Healing, Vol. 1.* E. Paul and C. Paul (trans). New York: Macmillan.

Janoff-Bulman, R. (1985) 'The aftermath of victimization: Rebuilding shattered assumptions.' In C. Figley (ed) *Trauma and its Wake.* New York: Brunner/Mazel.

Jennings, S. (ed) (1975) *Creative Therapy.* London: Pitman Publishing.

Jennings, S. (ed) (1987) *Dramatherapy: Theory and Practice for Teachers and Clinicians.* Beckenham, Kent: Croom Helm.

Jennings, S. (ed) (1993) *Play Therapy with Children: A Practitioner's Guide.* London: Blackwell Scientific.

Jennings, S. (ed) (1995) *Dramatherapy with Children and Adolescents.* London: Routledge.

Jennings, S. and Hickson, A. (2002) 'Pause for thought: Action or stillness with young people.' In A. Bannister and A. Huntington (eds) *Communicating with Children and Adolescents: Action for Change.* London: Jessica Kingsley Publishers.

Kagan, J. (1991) 'A conceptual analysis of the affect.' *Journal of the American Psychoanalytic Association 39*, 109–130.

Kahn, T. and Chambers, H. (1991) 'Assessing reoffense risk with juvenile sexual offenders.' *Child Welfare 70*, 333–345.

Kaprow, A. (1993) *Essays on the Blurring of Art and Life* (ed J. Kelley). Berkeley and Los Angeles: University of California Press.

Karp, M., Holmes, P. and Bradshaw-Tauvon, K. (1998) *The Handbook of Psychodrama.* London: Routledge.

Kazdin, A.E. (1994) 'Psychotherapy for children and adolescents.' In A.E. Bergin and S.L. Garfield (eds) *Handbook of Psychotherapy and Behavior Change* (4th edn). New York: Wiley.

Kellermann, P.F. and Hudgins, M.K. (eds) (2000) *Psychodrama with Trauma Survivors: Acting Out Your Pain.* London: Jessica Kingsley Publishers.

Kempe, C.H., Silverman, F.N., Steele, D.F., Droegemueller, W. and Wilver, H.K. (1962) 'The battered child syndrome.' *Journal of the American Medical Association 181*, 17–24.

Klein, M. (1975) *Collected Works, Vol. 1: Love, Guilt and Reparation.* London: Hogarth Press.

Kolb, L.C. (1987) 'Neurophysiological hypothesis explaining post-traumatic stress disorder.' *American Journal of Psychiatry 144*, 989–995.

Krystal, J.H., Kosten, T.R., Perry, B.D., Southwick, S., Mason, J.W. and Giller, E.L. (1989) 'Neurobiological aspects of PTSD: Review of clinical and preclinical studies.' *Behaviour Therapy 20*, 177–198.

Landis, J. (1956) 'Experiences of 500 children with adult sexual deviants.' *Psychiatric Quarterly Supplement 30*, 91–109.

Langer, K.G. (1992) 'Psychotherapy with the neuropsychologically impaired adult.' *American Journal of Psychotherapy 46*, 620–639.

Leichtman, M. (1992) 'Psychotherapeutic interventions with brain-injured children and their families: ii. Psychotherapy.' *Bulletin of the Menninger Clinic 56*, 338–360.

Lindberg, F.H. and Distad, L.J. (1985) 'Post-traumatic stress disorders in women who experienced childhood incest.' *Child Abuse and Neglect 9*, 329–334.

Lusk, R. and Waterman, J. (1986) 'Effects of sexual abuse on children.' In K. Macfarlane, J. Waterman, S. Conerly, L. Damon, M. Durfee and S. Long (eds) *Sexual Abuse of Young Children.* London: Holt, Rinehart and Winston.

Luxmoore, N. (2002) 'Can we do something? Young people using action methods to support each other in school.' In A. Bannister and A. Huntington (eds) *Communicating with Children and Adolescents: Action for Change.* London: Jessica Kingsley Publishers.

Lyle, J. and Holly, S. (1941) 'The therapeutic value of puppets.' *Bulletin of the Menninger Clinic 5*, 223–226.

Main, M. and Solomon, J. (1986) 'Discovery of an insecure-disorganised/disorientated attachment pattern: Procedures, findings and implications for the classification of behaviour.' In T.B. Brazelton and M.W. Yogman (eds) *Affective Development in Infancy*. Norwood, NJ: Ablex.

Maines, B. and Robinson, G. (1988) *B/G-Steem: A Self-esteem Scale with Locus of Control Items*. Bristol: Lucky Duck Publications.

Mehdi, P.R., Sen, M.D.P. and Sen, A.K. (1997) 'The effectiveness of psychodrama in changing the attitudes among depressed patients.' *The Journal of Personality and Clinical Studies 13*, 1–2, 19–23.

Miller, A. (1987) *For Your Own Good: The Roots of Violence in Child-Rearing*. London: Virago.

Mollon, P. (1996) *Multiple Selves, Multiple Voices: Working with Trauma, Violation and Dissociation*. Chichester: Wiley.

Moreno, J.L. (1977) *Psychodrama, 1st Volume* (5th edn) New York: Beacon House.

Moreno, J.L. (1993) *Who Shall Survive?* McLean, VA: ASGPP (Student edited, based on 2nd edn, 1953).

Moreno, J.L. and Moreno, F.B. (1944) *Spontaneity Theory of Child Development*. Psychodrama Monographs, No. 8. New York: Beacon House.

Moustakas, C. (1953) *Children in Play Therapy*. New York: McGraw Hill.

Naglieri, J.A., Le Buffe, P.A. and Pfeiffer, S.I. (1993) *Devereux Behaviour Rating Scale: School Form Manual*. San Antonio: Harcourt Brace and Co.

Newman, F. and Holzman, L. (1993) *Lev Vygotsky: Revolutionary Scientist*. London and New York: Routledge.

O'Callaghan, D. and Print, B. (1994) 'Adolescent sexual abusers: Research, assessment and treatment.' In T. Morrison, M. Erooga and R.C. Beckett (eds) *Sexual Offending Against Children: Assessment and Treatment of Male Abusers*. London and New York: Routledge.

Panksepp, J., Siviy, S.M. and Normansell, L.A. (1985) 'Brain opioids and social emotions.' In M. Reite and T. Field (eds) *The Psychobiology of Attachment and Separation*. Orlando, FL: Academic Press.

Parton, N. and Wattam, C. (1999) *Child Sexual Abuse: Responding to the Experiences of Children*. Chichester: Wiley/NSPCC.

Payne, H. (1993) 'Directory of arts therapies research.' In H. Payne (ed) *Handbook of Inquiry in the Arts Therapies: One River, Many Currents*. London: Jessica Kingsley Publishers.

Pearson, J. (ed) (1996) *Discovering the Self through Drama and Movement: The Sesame Approach*. London: Jessica Kingsley Publishers.

Pearson, Q.M. (1994) 'Treatment techniques for adult female survivors of childhood sexual abuse.' *Journal of Counseling and Development 73*, 1, 32–37.

Peters, S.D. (1988) 'Child sexual abuse and later psychological problems.' In G.E. Wyatt and G.J. Powell (eds) *Lasting Effects of Child Sexual Abuse*. London: Sage.

Piaget, J. and Inhelder, B. (1969) *The Psychology of the Child*. Trowbridge: Basic Books.

Pitzele, P. (1991) 'Adolescents inside out: Intrapsychic psychodrama.' In P. Holmes and M. Karp (eds) *Psychodrama, Inspiration and Technique*. London: Routledge.

Pomeroy, W. (1968) *Boys and Sex*. New York: Delacorte.

Prior, S. (1996) *Object Relations in Severe Trauma: Psychotherapy of the Sexually Abused Child*. New Jersey and London: Jason Aronson Inc.

Prodgers, A. (1984) 'Psychopathology of the physically abusing parent: A comparison with the borderline syndrome.' *International Journal of Child Abuse and Neglect 8*, 411–424.

Pynoos, R.S., Steinberg, A.M. and Goenjian, A. (1996) 'Traumatic stress in childhood and adolescence: Recent developments and current controversies.' In B.A. van der Kolk, A.C. Mcfarlane and L. Weisaeth (eds) *Traumatic Stress: The Effects of Overwhelming Experience on Mind, Body and Society.* London and New York: The Guilford Press.

Ragsdale, K.G., Cox, R.D., Finn, P. and Eisler, R.M. (1996) 'Effectiveness of short-term specialized inpatient treatment for war-related Post Traumatic Stress Disorder: A role for adventure-based counseling and psychodrama.' *Journal of Traumatic Stress 9*, 2, 269–283.

Ramey, J. (1979) 'Dealing with the last taboo.' *SEICUS 7*, 1–2, 6–7.

Rapkin, A.J., James, L.D., Darke, L.L., Stampler, F.M. and Naliboff, B.D. (1990) 'History of physical and sexual abuse in women with chronic pelvic pain.' *Obstetric Gynaecology 76*, 92.

Reiter, R.C. and Gambone, J.C. (1989) 'Demographic and historical variables in women with idiopathic chronic pelvic pain.' *Obstetric Gynaecology 75*, 428–432.

Richardson, S. and Bacon, H. (eds) (2001) *Creative Responses to Child Sexual Abuse: Challenges and Dilemmas.* London: Jessica Kingsley Publishers.

Rimsza, M.E., Berg, R.A. and Locke, C. (1988) 'Sexual abuse: Somatic and emotional reactions.' *Child Abuse and Neglect 12*, 201–208.

Rogers, C.M. and Terry, T. (1984) 'Clinical intervention with boy victims of sexual abuse.' In I. Stuart and J. Greer (eds) *Victims of Sexual Aggression.* New York: Van Nostrand Reinhold.

Rogers, C.R. (1951) *Client Centered Therapy.* London: Constable.

Ruiz Lazaro, P.M., Velilla Picazo, J.M. and Bonals Pi, A. (1996) 'Psychodrama group therapy in school children from an infantile psychiatric unit.' (Spanish) *Revista de Psiquiatria Infanto-Juvenil 3*, 207–211.

Rutter, M. (1981) *Maternal Deprivation Re-assessed.* Harmondsworth: Penguin Books.

Ryan, G. and Lane, S. (eds) (1991) *Juvenile Sexual Offending – Causes, Consequences and Corrections.* Lexington, MA: Lexington Books.

Ryan, G., Lane, S., Davis, J. and Isaac, C. (1987) 'Juvenile sex offenders: Development and correction.' *Child Abuse and Neglect 11*, 385–395.

Sanderson, C. (1995) *Counselling Adult Survivors of Child Sexual Abuse* (2nd edn). London: Jessica Kingsley Publishers.

Saxe, G., Chinman, G., Berkovitz, R., Hall, K., Lieberg, G., Schwartz, J. and van der Kolk, B.A. (1994) 'Somatization in patients with dissociative disorders.' *American Journal of Psychiatry 151*, 1329–1335.

Scarinci, I.C., McDonald-Haile, J., Bradley, L.A. and Richter, J.E. (1994) 'Altered pain perception and psychosocial features among women with gastrointestinal disorders and history of abuse: A preliminary model.' *American Journal of Medicine 97*, 108–118.

Schacht, A.J., Kerlinsky, D. and Carlson, C. (1990) 'Group therapy with sexually abused boys: Leadership, Projective identification and countertransference issues.' *International Journal of Group Psychotherapy 40*, 4, 401–417.

Schechter, M.D. and Roberge, L. (1976) 'Sexual exploitation.' In R.E. Helfer and C.H. Kempe (eds) *Child Abuse and Neglect: The Family and the Community.* Cambridge, MA: Ballinger.

Schore, A.N. (1994) *Affect Regulation and the Origin of the Self.* Hillsdale, NJ, and Hove: Lawrence Erlbaum.

Schore, A.N. (1997a) *The Neurodevelopmental Aspects of Projective Identification.* Paper presented at Psychoanalysis in Clinical Social Work National Conference, Seattle, WA.

Schore, A.N. (1997b) 'Early organization of the non-linear right brain and development of a predilection to psychiatric diseases.' *Developmental Psychopathology 9,* 4, 559–631.

Sgroi, S.M. (1982) *Handbook of Clinical Intervention in Child Sexual Abuse.* Lexington, MA: Lexington Books.

Sheldon, H. and Bannister, A. (1992) 'Working with adult female survivors of childhood sexual abuse.' In A. Bannister (ed) *From Hearing to Healing: Working with the Aftermath of Child Sexual Abuse.* Harlow, Essex: Longman.

Skuse, D., Bentovim, A., Hodges, J., Stevenson, J., Andreou, C., Lanyada, M., New, M., Williams, B. and McMillan, D. (1998) 'Risk factors for development of sexually abusive behaviour in sexually victimized adolescent boys: Cross sectional study.' *British Medical Journal 317*, 175–179.

Slade, P. (1995) *Childplay: Its Importance for Human Development.* London: Jessica Kingsley Publishers.

Smith, C. and Woodhead, K. (1999) 'Justice for children.' In N. Parton and C. Wattam *Child Sexual Abuse: Responding to the Experiences of Children.* Chichester: Wiley/NSPCC.

Smith, G. (2002) 'Freeing the self: Using psychodrama techniques with children and adolescents who stammer.' In A. Bannister and A. Huntington (eds) *Communicating with Children and Adolescents: Action for Change.* London: Jessica Kingsley Publishers.

Spanos, N. (1994) 'Multiple identity enactments and multiple personality disorder: A sociocognitive perspective.' *Psychological Bulletin 116*, 143–165.

Steele, B.F. and Alexander, H. (1981) 'Long-term effects of sexual abuse in childhood.' In P.B. Mrazek and C.H. Kempe (eds) *Sexually Abused Children and their Families.* New York: Pergamon Press.

Stern, D.N. (2002) *The First Relationship.* Cambridge, MA, and London: Harvard University Press.

Summit, R. (1983) 'The child sexual abuse accommodation syndrome.' *Child Abuse and Neglect 7*, 177–193.

Terr, L. (1988) 'What happens to early memories of trauma? A study of twenty children under age five at the time of documented traumatic events.' *Journal of the American Academy of Child and Adolescent Psychiatry 27*, 96–104.

Toomey, T.C., Hernandez, J.T., Gittelman, D.F. and Hulka, J.F. (1993) 'Relationship of sexual and physical abuse to pain and psychological assessment variables in chronic pelvic pain patients.' *Pain 53*, 105–109.

Tsai, M., Feldman-Summers, S. and Edgar, M. (1979) 'Childhood molestation: Variables related to differential impacts of psychosexual functioning in adult women.' *Journal of Abnormal Psychology 88*, 407–417.

Turner, S.W., McFarlane, A.C. and van der Kolk, B.A. (1996) 'The therapeutic environment and new explorations in the treatment of post-traumatic stress disorder.' In B.A. van der Kolk, A.C. McFarlane and L. Weisaeth (eds) *Traumatic Stress: The Effects of Overwhelming Experience on Mind, Body and Society.* New York and London: The Guilford Press.

van der Kolk, B.A. (1996) 'The complexity of adaptation to trauma.' In B.A. van der Kolk, A.C. Mcfarlane and L. Weisaeth (eds) *Traumatic Stress: The Effects of Overwhelming Experience on Mind, Body and Society.* New York and London: The Guilford Press.

van der Kolk, B.A., Mcfarlane, A.C. and Weisaeth, L. (eds) (1996) *Traumatic Stress: The Effects of Overwhelming Experience on Mind, Body and Society.* New York and London: The Guilford Press.

van der Kolk, B.A, Perry, C. and Herman, J.L. (1991) 'Childhood origins of self-destructive behaviour.' *American Journal of Psychiatry 148*, 1665–1671.

van der Kolk, B.A., Roth, S., Pelcovitz, D. and Mandel, F. (1993) *Disorders of Extreme Stress: Results of the DSM-IV Field Trials for PTSD.* Washington, DC: American Psychiatric Association.

Vygotsky, L. (1934; reprinted 1962) *Thought and Language.* Cambridge, MA: MIT Press.

Vygotsky, L. (1978) *Mind in Society.* Cambridge, MA: Harvard University Press.

Walker, E., Katon, W., Harrop-Griffiths, J., Holm, L., Russo, J. and Hickok, L.R. (1988) 'Relationship of chronic pelvic pain to psychiatric diagnoses and childhood sexual abuse.' *American Journal of Psychiatry 145*, 75–79.

Waller, G. (1994) 'Childhood sexual abuse and borderline personality disorder in the eating disorders.' *Child Abuse and Neglect 18*, 97–101.

Waller, G., Ruddock, A. and Cureton, S. (1995) 'Cognitive correlates of reported sexual abuse in eating-disordered women.' *Journal of Interpersonal Violence 10*, 176–187.

Warner, M. (1994) *From the Beast to the Blonde: On Fairytales and their Tellers.* London: Chatto and Windus.

West, J. (1992) *Child-Centred Play Therapy.* London: Edward Arnold.

Wilson, K., Kendrick, P. and Ryan, V. (1992) *Play Therapy: A Non-directive Approach for Children and Adolescents.* London: Bailliere Tindall.

Winn, L. (1994) *Post-traumatic Stress Disorder and Dramatherapy.* London: Jessica Kingsley Publishers.

Winnicott, D.W. (1964) *The Child, the Family, and the Outside World.* Harmondsworth: Penguin.

Winnicott, D.W. (1971; reprinted 1974 and 1996) *Playing and Reality.* London: Tavistock, Harmondsworth: Pelican; London: Routledge.

Woltman, A.G. (1943) 'Puppetry as a means of psychotherapy.' In R.B. Wynn *Encyclopaedia of Child Guidance.* New York: Philosophical Library.

Woodhead, M. (1997) 'Psychology and the cultural construction of children's needs.' In A. James and A. Prout (eds) *Constructing and Reconstructing Childhood.* London: Falmer Press.

Wyre, R. (2000) 'Paedophile characteristics and patterns of behaviour: Developing a typology.' In C. Itzin (ed) *Home Truths about Child Sexual Abuse: Influencing Policy and Practice – A Reader.* London: Routledge.

Young, L. (1992) 'Sexual abuse and the problem of embodiment.' *Child Abuse and Neglect 16,* 89–100.

Subject Index

Author Index